JERRY BRUCKHEIMER
FILMS

JERRY BRUCKHEIMER

WHEN LIGHTNING STRIKES | FOUR DECADES OF FILMMAKING

FOREWORD BY **JOHNNY DEPP** | WRITTEN BY **MICHAEL SINGER**

Disney EDITIONS

New York • Los Angeles

FOREWORD BY JOHNNY DEPP

Back in 2009, I approached Jerry with six photographs. These six photographs depicted a sickly, grizzled type character with curious black lines dripping down across his noble face and a dead bird perched on his head, his back adorned with treasures that a live bird might deposit. Jerry took one look at these photographs and said, "Let's do it!"

Now, most producers would have had you physically removed from the premises at the very thought of such a thing, but I suppose what is so uniquely special for me, aside from taking such a giant leap of faith on the crazed fruit of my inner ravings is that Jerry is the only guy I know who could make such a movie. And as we all know, that makes all the difference.

As the book you hold here will shortly tell you, Jerry's early days were a decidedly humble affair. His ever burgeoning rise is a salute to hard work and perseverance: an inspiration to entrepreneurs everywhere. Furthermore, my admiration for the ethical way in which he embodies the nature of his vocation is infinite.

By the time of our first collaboration, Jerry had long achieved legendary status. Of course, I was aware of his prominence, but it wasn't until *Pirates of the Caribbean: The Curse of the Black Pearl* that I had the chance to witness those famed abilities firsthand. After the magnanimous Dick Cook offered me the prized role, the film suffered from a troubled genesis on set. Certain folks at Disney, whom we shall favor at this juncture by forgetting their names, were less than impressed by my portrayal of Captain Jack Sparrow. This executive peanut gallery further piped up with such cerebral nuggets as "is he drunk?", "is he gay?", "why does he have to walk like that?" The situation was looking bleak. Clearly, the studio wanted me out. The director, my friend Gore Verbinski, stood firmly by my side, but it was going to take the talents of a man who wielded a weight far greater than the combined sum of our lowly stock to keep me from catching the early bus home. Jerry proceeded to work his wonders on the studio, standing firm against the barrage of protest for the bizarre choices of a lowly actor. The rest, as they say, is . . . whatever it is.

However, it must be said that, more than just a brother in the face of battle behind the silver screen, Jerry has become both a dear friend and treasured confidant. I believe that in the smarter states they measure the caliber of his advice by gold bullion.

Over his peerless career, Jerry has more than made his mark on Hollywood. He is one of the greatest producers this town has ever seen. I count myself fortunate to have been able to peddle my wares in the grand age of Jerry Bruckheimer, and I invite you now, dear reader, to sample that age, which, make no mistake, continues to hurtle along at full pelt without any sign of slowing, and perhaps take a modicum of that trademark Bruckheimer vision, verve, and vitality home with you.

Have faith, for I plan on doing the same and fully suspect that such attributes will prove to serve us both well.

Johnny Depp

Los Angeles | September 2012

INTRODUCTION BY JERRY BRUCKHEIMER

I never imagined that there would someday be a book about me. That's probably because I never imagined I could actually become a movie producer, particularly one who would warrant such attention. Growing up in humble surroundings in Detroit, the only child of German immigrant parents, I wouldn't even dare to imagine something so far-fetched. Like most kids in my neighborhood, I was preoccupied with more typical matters, like sports, getting passing grades in school, and saving enough money to buy new hockey cards.

But there was one place where I allowed myself to dream big: inside the Mercury Theater, our local single-screen movie house at 6 Mile and Schaefer.

That's where I fell in love with movies. And nothing was ever the same after that. It was hard to believe that I could spend a few hours in a darkened theater and come out completely transformed. How exciting it was to watch those flickering images which magically imitated, but were better than, life itself. How thrilling it would be to actually make that happen.

Now, to my utter amazement, both dreams have come true. This success didn't happen overnight. It took a lot of hard work and perseverance with a little luck thrown in. Or, as the saying goes, "The harder I worked, the luckier I got."

I'm so honored to share this book with you, the audience for whom I've made the films and television programs which I've been lucky enough to produce over four decades. Hopefully, some of the images will bring back memories of where you were, and who you were with, when you first saw *Flashdance* or *Top Gun*, *Pirates of the Caribbean* or *The Lone Ranger*, and all the other movies in between. We all have our own personal memories of watching films, but for me the shared experience is what I love the best.

Attending Hollywood screenings has never been my first choice. Instead, I prefer to spend the time in a neighborhood theater with my wife, Linda, where we are surrounded by hundreds of other movie fans. We love to get a bucket of popcorn and a Coca-Cola and listen to the crowd laugh or cry or scream in delight. After all, these are the people that I produce movies for. It is their energy that fills me with excitement and continues to inspire me.

Many decades later, I get the same thrill as I did as a ten-year-old, when the heroes and heroines on that movie screen looked larger than life, when each story brought a sense of wonder and delight and purpose to my young life. These are experiences that I savor to this day. These are the emotional peaks that keep me constantly moving forward.

Along with the movies, my other great love was, and still is, photography. When I was six years old, a new chapter of my life opened up when my uncle, Eric, presented me with a mysterious object called a camera . . . that's pretty young for second chapters, but that beautiful little plastic and metal box changed my life. Looking through the viewfinder was like peering into another world, one which I could control with my own eye. In many of my own childhood pictures, you could see the camera looped around my neck, ready for action. And I took photos of everything—from ordinary household objects to friends and family.

And that tradition continues on. For several decades I have snapped pictures on the sets of almost all the movies I've produced. In the pages of this book are a small representation of these photos, freeze-frame fragments from the Pirates of the Caribbean movies, *Pearl Harbor*, and *Black Hawk Down*. These are the angles and moments that have caught my eye behind-the-scenes, from the iconic images to the candid shots of the cast and crew.

I am very fortunate to have lived my dreams and am grateful to the millions of movie lovers around the world for allowing our films into their lives.

I am also deeply indebted to the brilliant actors, directors, writers, cinematographers, crew members, studio executives, as well as my talented team at JBF and JBTV, who are all part of this huge collaborative effort. They manage to make the hard work involved in creating movies and television so satisfying and fun. It doesn't hurt matters that I have worked with some of the very best in this industry. We all share the love of this art, as well as the belief that we are involved in the most exciting business in the world.

My father, who worked in the same men's clothing store for over thirty years, gave me this advice when I was very young. He said: "Don't get a job where you spend your time counting the days until your two-week vacation."

And that was the very best guidance he could have given me. I ended up following my dreams and working hard to make them a reality. The very fact that, against every expectation, my own dreams came true means that yours can too.

So, in the words of Captain Jack Sparrow, "Now, bring me that horizon. . . ."

Jerry Bruckheimer

Los Angeles | March 2013

JERRY BRUCKHEIMER PHOTOGRAPHER

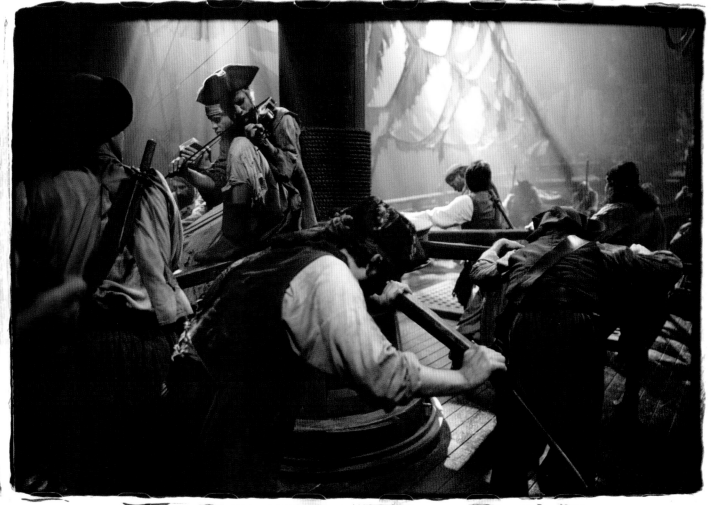

"ALL I EVER WANTED WAS TO MAKE MOVIES"

JERRY BRUCKHEIMER:
THE MAN WHO FOUND IT AT THE MOVIES
"LIGHTNING SYMBOLIZES HOW AN IDEA CAN REALLY SPARK SOMETHING SPECIAL." | JERRY BRUCKHEIMER

In Hollywood, one of the greatest honors that can be bestowed upon one of its own is, ironically, to have them plant their hands and feet in wet concrete. This somewhat sinister scenario takes on a different meaning when it's understood that such markings are for the entrance area of the legendary Grauman's Chinese Theatre on Hollywood Boulevard, where, since 1927, industry icons have identified themselves in such a fashion for the perusal and fascination of millions. This promenade leading up to one of the few remaining temples of film and glamour in Hollywood is a sacred place for movie fans the world over, who come to worship at what essentially is a shrine to the gods of cinema.

And so it was, in the early, unseasonably drizzly evening of Monday, May 17, 2010, another Hollywood legend was invited to join his predecessors in becoming an immortal. What made the invitation rather unusual was that it was for one of the relatively few nonmovie stars of the nearly 200 celebrities who preceded him, a true recognition of the import and impact of the one being feted. Instead, it

was for a man who makes stars—Jerry Bruckheimer. The occasion was made even more special by not only the fact that the most recent production from Jerry Bruckheimer Films at the time, *Prince of Persia: The Sands of Time*, was having its Hollywood premiere at the Chinese; but also that the evening included "A Cinematic Celebration of Jerry Bruckheimer," in which five of the producer's best-loved films were being screened and introduced by several of their stars and directors. Attending the ceremony in support of the man they had worked for and with through the decades was a veritable pantheon of stars whose careers were often profoundly affected by his influence, including Tom Cruise, Eddie Murphy, Bruce Willis, Nicolas Cage, Sir Ben Kingsley, Jake Gyllenhaal, Jon Voight, Kelly McGillis, Jonathan Pryce, Justin Bartha, Billy Bob Thornton, Michael Clarke Duncan, and Tom Skerritt, among others; and, from the other side of the camera, filmmakers Tony Scott, Jon Turteltaub, and Mike Newell showed up as well. First Cruise, and then Cage, each of them catapulted to megastardom

by Bruckheimer, sincerely praised the producer from the podium as a great talent and stalwart friend.

". . . We're here to celebrate the greatest producer, I think in modern history," said a casually attired Cruise before the assembled Hollywood Boulevard crowd and video cameras. "There's a letter that I read that Mark Twain wrote to his daughter, who was asking for his advice on how to tell a story. At the end of it, he said, 'For God's sake, always make the most entertaining choice.' And I think that, to me, really represents who Jerry Bruckheimer is . . . he's there to entertain us."

A more formally dressed Cage followed by confirming and expanding upon Cruise's thoughts. "We're here to celebrate the great entertainer, Jerry Bruckheimer—a true movie enthusiast who makes movies that he wants to see. He always watches movies with the public, with the popcorn, and at the theater. Perhaps this is why his films appeal to all people all over the world, no matter their race or beliefs. He knows what the audience needs, because their wants are his wants—to be entertained and happy. . . . Jerry has always been there for me; he is not a fair-weather friend. He loves his actors and is intensely loyal to us. When Hollywood is fickle on its stars, Jerry isn't. He's there for us, a fan who believes in his actors and supports us through good times and bad times. . . . You make people happy, and in this day and age, how can that be anything but the right thing to do?"

Bruckheimer himself then stepped to the podium, and this coolest of customers seemed almost daunted by the gravity of the moment. Speaking in a voice touched by emotion, as his wife, Linda, and daughter, Alexandra, along with a bevy of celebrities sat nearby, he began, "This is one of the most exciting moments of my career. To be alongside some of Hollywood's greatest talent is such an honor. I'm humbled by it, and I can't comprehend it. The irony is, this is where it all started for me—at a theater back in Detroit, in kind of a modest neighborhood. I fell in love with what was on that big screen. I wanted to be part of it. I had dreams and aspirations for it, but that's not enough. You have to have great people around you to do that. I can't thank the great writers, directors, actors, studio executives, and technicians enough. They're such a big part of this honor. I thank you from the bottom of my heart for being there for me and teaching me the way.

"I'd also like to acknowledge the fans and the moviegoers," continued the producer, "because without you, the theaters are empty and I'm on the unemployment lines. So, my heart goes out to you, and I hope I can inspire you the way these great filmmakers around me inspired me."

Unable to attend due to filming in Venice (Italy, not Southern California), another actor whose career forever changed as a result of starring in a Jerry Bruckheimer movie, placed a full-page advertisement in that day's issue of the industry bible, *Variety*:

Dear Jerry,
Congratulations on this, your latest in a seemingly
infinite line of illustrious accolades!!! Your
renown remains unsurpassed. It is an honor
to call you both colleague and friend.
With love, respect, and profound thanks,
Johnny & Captain Jack Sparrow

And while Bruckheimer's latest extravaganza played to an appreciative audience inside of the main Chinese theater, enthusiasts in the adjacent Mann Chinese 6 multiplex delighted in rewatching on the big screen the likes of *Pirates of the Caribbean*: *The Curse of the Black Pearl, Armageddon, National Treasure, Top Gun,* and *Beverly Hills Cop.* Those films, however, were only five out of a truly staggering output over a producing career which, two years from that date, would commemorate its fortieth year.

THE VISIONARY

Although the familiar adage states that lightning doesn't strike twice, for Jerry Bruckheimer it has struck a multitude of times. And each time, it's another notch on an ever-lengthening belt, which has now stretched back through four decades of almost supernatural success.

This unprecedented creative streak is full of films and television shows that are both familiar, and in some cases, surprising. While there are better-known Bruckheimer productions—such as *Flashdance*; *Beverly Hills Cop* and *Beverly Hills Cop II*; *Top Gun*; *Bad Boys* and *Bad Boys II*; *Crimson Tide*; *The Rock*; *Con Air*; *Armageddon*; *Enemy of the State*; *Remember the Titans*; *Pearl Harbor*; *Black Hawk Down*; the Pirates of the Caribbean films; and the National Treasure films, plus TV's three CSI programs, *Cold Case*; *Without a Trace*; and *The Amazing Race*—earlier in his

career, he was also a force behind such films as *American Gigolo*; *Cat People*; *Farewell, My Lovely*; and *Thief.* His films have either made, consolidated, or reinvented the images of Johnny Depp, Tom Cruise, Nicolas Cage, Richard Gere, Eddie Murphy, Will Smith, Ben Affleck, Denzel Washington, Keira Knightley, Martin Lawrence, Jake Gyllenhaal, and Armie Hammer. Actors with smaller roles in Bruckheimer's films have also gone on to great success following their experiences with the producer, including Tom Hardy (*Black Hawk Down*), Ryan Gosling (*Remember the Titans*), Zach Galifianakis (*G-Force*), Eric Bana (*Black Hawk Down*), and Ed Helms (*Confessions of a Shopaholic*).

In terms of his impact on the motion picture and television industries, from a world box office perspective, it's not only fair, but probably undeniable, to say that Bruckheimer is the most successful producer in the history of both mediums. Bruckheimer's films and television shows have not only influenced popular culture, but, in some cases, defined it. And although cinema is usually considered a director's medium—and Bruckheimer is well known to be completely respectful of their visions on his productions—as a producer, he has an indelible, creative stamp that hearkens back to the days of such strong, hands-on pioneers as David O. Selznick, Darryl F. Zanuck, Sam Spiegel, and, for that matter, Walt Disney. These were fearless pioneers who were unafraid to go, and go big, when the situation or subject matter warranted that approach.

Perhaps the visionary whom Bruckheimer most closely resembles is Cecil B. DeMille, who staunchly made epic films for mass audiences on a grand scale, pioneering visual effects and other new technologies, and then brilliantly marketing his movies with ballyhoo to maximum excitement. Like DeMille—and more than any other contemporary producer—Jerry Bruckheimer has not only become a household name, but an actual brand.

Bruckheimer's approach to filmmaking has, appropriately enough, echoed words written by his favorite screenwriter, Robert Bolt (*Lawrence of Arabia, Doctor Zhivago, A Man for All Seasons*) who, in a letter dated March 7, 1973, to the author (then a twenty-year-old college newspaper movie critic) wrote: "Film and Theatre are both Popular Arts. In the long run they cannot continue without a mass audience. If a writer does not like the mass audience, or has things to say which he cannot make available to the understanding of a mass audience, then he should not write for Film or Theatre. . . . Such a man should write essays or novels or philosophical treatises. He should not write unintelligible films or plays, or plays and films which are unintelligible to a popular audience. . . . [Critics] have now made the illogical assumption that any film which entertains must necessarily lack any other value. And they have almost assumed that a film which does not entertain but which carries a number of intellectually fashionable references must necessarily be of value.

"The assumption that entertaining films are shallow is a self-fulfilling prophecy," concluded Bolt in his letter. "The gap between the 'entertainment film' and the 'art film' is widening; we are approaching a situation in which entertainment and art are seen to be incompatible or even hostile and that spells the death of any popular art."

Jerry Bruckheimer's decidedly and intentionally populist films have never pretended to be "intellectually fashionable," but have always tried to be, first and foremost, great entertainments. Their biggest fans have certainly been a part of the mass audience to which Bolt refers, precisely because they were made to be intelligible to as wide a range of viewers as possible. And while Bruckheimer's films have occasionally suffered the critical slings and arrows of which

Bolt wrote, more astute critical assessments have been present from the start. It's been all too easy for lazier critics and pundits to pigeonhole the producer as simply a guy who makes action movies in which lots of things explode, but that's a deeply inaccurate representation of the entire range of subject matter and style in Bruckheimer's oeuvre.

More accurate was *Time* magazine journalist Desa Philadelphia's assessment in the publication's "2004 Time 100": "Hollywood preview audiences cheer when his name sprawls across the screen. People ask for his autograph in airports. Producer Jerry Bruckheimer has become the outsize star of his own Hollywood story. His hip, high-voltage action films of the '90s (*Con Air, Bad Boys, Armageddon*) established a new style for the Hollywood blockbuster and helped make superstars of Ben Affleck, Nicolas Cage, and Will Smith. Last year, with *Pirates of the Caribbean*, he even managed to mainstream reluctant celebrity Johnny Depp. Rare in the entertainment world, he has been able to transfer his instinct for the mass audience from movies to television, creating the hit crime-investigation franchise CSI and a seemingly endless parade of spin-offs and imitators like *Without a Trace*. All told, Bruckheimer's feature film projects have grossed more than $13 billion. He has done it by showing that commercial entertainment can be big and brawny but not entirely brainless. Bruckheimer says he simply makes 'what I like.' Which is why people cheer Jerry Bruckheimer: he likes what they like."

Other critics as of late have been kinder to Bruckheimer's now archetypal films, particularly when comparing them to latter-day imitators who draw from the well, but fail to create films as beautifully crafted as the ones from which they were derived. But the truth is that Bruckheimer has never put much stock in critical appraisal, one way

or the other. "If I made movies for critics, I'd be living in a small Hollywood apartment," he told *The New York Times*' Laura M. Holson in 2003. "Art is in the eyes of the beholder. If you love it and the critics hate it, does that mean you are wrong? I don't think so."

The importance of the signature Bruckheimer look in establishing the producer's success was explained by The Script Lab (www.thescriptlab.com), a Web site dedicated to screenwriting, in an article entitled "The Bruckheimer Blueprint": "You've seen his movies, you've watched his television, you've probably even bought into his brand. His name . . . Jerry Bruckheimer, and in movie terms he is God. Arguably the most successful producer of the last three generations, Jerry Bruckheimer is synonymous with blockbuster success. . . . Clearly, Bruckheimer is the maestro, but why? What does he know that we don't? What's his secret? His blueprint for success? Answer: DESIGN. Almost all American business underestimates the consumer's desire for design. It's not so much how great a product is—it is how it looks. Apple didn't invent the MP3 player technology, yet it's the king of the MP3 player market. Why? Apple just designed a better device: the iPod. Apple "invented" how it looked. And Bruckheimer does the same thing in film and television. . . . Every major police department has its own CSI units, but do they look like Bruckheimer's CSI lab environments? The facilities, the technology, the style . . . not even close to reality, but it sure looks cool. So we buy into it, and then we're hooked."

Bruckheimer's success is proof positive that "popular art," contrary to Bolt's fears, is alive and well. His films not only rate as popular art, but certainly in the cases of such '80s benchmarks as *Flashdance, Top Gun*, and *Beverly Hills Cop*, are actual pop art, creating a specific cinematic iconography no less valid than those created on canvas. Believing that there's room for true artistry in mass commercial films, Bruckheimer has consistently employed the top visualists in their fields, including brilliant directors, cinematographers, production designers, art directors and set decorators, and others engaged in the myriad pieces of the overall puzzle that result in a feature film or television program.

Further proof of Jerry Bruckheimer's accomplishments in creating popular entertainment is in the numbers. In addition to his films' worldwide revenues, (the Pirates of the Caribbean films alone have, to date, taken in more than $3.6 billion globally), he had a record-breaking ten series on network television in the 2005–2006 season, a feat unprecedented in nearly sixty years of television history. Every week, it's estimated that a staggering 240 million people in the U.S. and around the world watch Jerry Bruckheimer Television programs.

His films (nineteen of which have exceeded the $100 million mark in U.S. box office receipts) and television programs have been acknowledged with a raft of awards: Oscars, Emmys, Grammys, Golden Globes, People's Choice, BAFTA (British Academy of Film and Television Arts), MTV, etc. The full panoply of ego-tickling kudos has descended upon Jerry Bruckheimer like cherry blossoms in April. Then, of course, there are his consistent seats of honor on the annual magazine lists of "Most Powerful," "Most Influential," and "New Establishment," year after year, and such media-friendly appellations as "Mr. Blockbuster," "Mega-Producer," and "Über-Producer."

As for Bruckheimer, he sees himself another way: "People think that producing is about big cigars and martinis. But I'm just a guy with a script tucked under his arm trying to get a movie made." Despite his exalted place in the show business pantheon, the essential task, Bruckheimer notes, is always the same—that long, often painful,

Sisyphean process of pushing a project uphill to fruition.

In interviews, or when speaking to students, Bruckheimer is constantly asked the same question: what's the magic formula explaining his monumental track record?

Bruckheimer's answer is always the same, and almost maddeningly simple: "I make movies and TV shows that I want to see."

The initial response to such a plain-spoken answer might be that, like Bruckheimer's disarming Cheshire catlike smile, he's hiding some ineffable secret, which, once released, will drain its keeper of his powers, or have his recipe stolen by a rival chef.

More likely, it's really just as simple as Jerry Bruckheimer states. The "magic" lies in the man's ability to connect his output to his own tastes, absolutely without compromise, and the fact that the producer's tastes echo those of the better part of the worldwide population. When Bruckheimer describes himself as a "meat and potatoes guy," he's noting a trait that applies to the majority of filmgoers around the world, whether their own meat and potatoes are all-American burgers and fries, French steak and pommes frites, or Japanese nikujaga stew. It's all about the basics, and to Jerry Bruckheimer—and those millions of moviegoers—that means story. "You always have to start with a strong story," Bruckheimer states emphatically, "and everything builds from that. Without that foundation, the rest is meaningless."

That's how Jerry Bruckheimer sees himself—as a storyteller, albeit on film rather than the printed page. And even with the visceral and highly kinetic style for which the producer has become famous (and which he pioneered), the clear reason for his success is that his output is accessible in such a way that it cuts across borders, cultures, education levels, and languages. In other words, he gives proof to the adage

that film truly is an international language. "I feel like I'm a producer who makes movies for the common man," he told an interviewer in 2001. "Movies are not only for the highbrow or the lowbrow, but for people in the middle who like to be entertained."

Perhaps that's why, by this point in time, forty years after receiving his first on-screen producing credit, Jerry Bruckheimer is a name that's equally as well known in London, Paris, Tokyo, and Sydney as it is in Hollywood. This in and of itself is a remarkable accomplishment, as few in his field are ever recognizable to a worldwide audience.

His famous "golden gut," as *The Washington Post* once referred to Bruckheimer's instinctive sense, has somehow plugged him right into the main circuit of the zeitgeist from one decade to the next. "If something doesn't make sense to Jerry, it's probably a good guess that it won't make sense to an audience," says Jerry Bruckheimer Films President Mike Stenson. "He has an absolute sixth sense about what works in a movie, and what doesn't. And if Jerry's name is going to be on a movie, then it has to be an A-list production in every department."

Says Chad Oman, JBF's president of production, "The thing that's interesting about Jerry is that he always looks at the big picture. From the beginning of developing a story or a concept, he's already on multiple tracks: who's the audience? What will the poster look like? How do I sell this movie? Jerry also knows every aspect of filmmaking."

"Jerry is extremely involved in everything that's going on, but he lets you do your thing," observes Jonathan Littman, president of Jerry Bruckheimer Television. "He gives you a lot of space and doesn't micromanage. All of the executives here operate with the feeling that even if they do make a mistake, they're not going to get yelled at or fired. It makes it easier to do your job. Jerry is also open to debate . . . but he's rarely wrong."

Adds KristieAnne Reed, onetime executive assistant to Bruckheimer, who is now the executive vice president of Jerry Bruckheimer Television, "Jerry works very hard. I know that sounds like a simple formula for success, but he always says to find great writers to tell great stories, and support them wherever they need to be supported. Jerry still reads every script and watches every cut of every episode of every series we do, even in the thirteenth season of *CSI*. He weighs in on every major casting decision and the list goes on and on . . . he doesn't cut corners. He does the work."

Notes Pat Sandston, who heads Bruckheimer's postproduction department and is associate producer on his films, "Jerry has a particular genius for finding a film's voice." And Executive Vice President Melissa Reid proffers, "In a business with huge amounts of money at stake and fragile egos on the line, you can't underestimate the value of having a strong captain at the helm of the ship. Jerry is a calm, confident, and stabilizing presence . . . he's like the eye of the storm. Each film presents a unique set of challenges and problems, but Jerry never gets rattled. His unflappable demeanor settles everyone around him and enables them to focus on their work and move toward the finish line."

THE "TEAM MANAGER"

When pressed for a definition of "producer," Bruckheimer couches it in sports terminology. "The easiest way to understand it," he notes, "is that in any sport there's a coach and a manager. Producers are the managers. We don't own the team, but we hire the players—the actors—and the coach—the director—and then manage the game."

Rob Marshall—Bruckheimer and Depp's choice of director for *Pirates of the Caribbean: On Stranger Tides*, the fourth entry of the blockbuster franchise—also

pondered the producer's modus operandi shortly before the release of the film in May 2011: "Jerry is so unique because he's the real thing. He's a producer's producer. He's so elegant and supportive, and so there for you. He really defines what a producer does, and it's not always like that. When I met Jerry, he said, 'For me, it's about surrounding myself with great people and artists.'"

Despite his reputation as a relentless propagator of high-concept filmmaking, Bruckheimer in actuality has continually defied expectations. "I try to figure out what everybody else is doing," states the producer, "and then not do it. I know that if there's a trend, I'll stay away from it. By the time the film opens, everything will be different. We try to find projects that are untrendy, that you can put a twist on to."

This penchant for out-of-the-box thinking has also led Bruckheimer to consistently, and unconventionally, cast stars against type and forever change their cinematic profiles. Some of the better examples of these alchemical transformations are comedian Eddie Murphy as a Detroit cop in the Beverly Hills Cop films; comic/rapper Will Smith and comedian Martin Lawrence as Miami cops in the Bad Boys opuses; the offbeat, quirky, and uncategorizable Nicolas Cage, remade as an action star in *The Rock* and six subsequent Bruckheimer productions; Australian comedian Eric Bana, made over as a hard-bitten Delta Force operator in *Black Hawk Down*; art house favorite Johnny Depp creating one of the most iconic characters in motion-picture history, as Captain Jack Sparrow in the Pirates of the Caribbean quartet; and Jake Gyllenhaal getting an action-hero makeover in *Prince of Persia: The Sands of Time*.

Throughout his career, Jerry Bruckheimer has always employed directors either already at the top of their games (Ridley Scott, Rob Marshall, Mike Newell),

or, even more often, at a relatively early stage of their careers (Michael Bay, Tony Scott, Gore Verbinski, Jon Turteltaub, Paul Schrader, Michael Mann, Martin Brest), sling-shotting them to greater fortune through their collaborations with the producer. "I've always liked working with directors who have a strong vision," he notes, "and [who are] bold enough to get it on-screen."

Bruckheimer has also advanced the use of music in his productions, whether that music comes in the form of an instrumental score or a sound track comprised of rock-and-roll tracks. He has employed such noted composer-musicians as Giorgio Moroder, Harold Faltermeyer, Hans Zimmer, and Trevor Rabin, all of whom have had rock or pop careers in addition to writing film music. The producer's films have also rolled out an impressive number of hit singles, including "Call Me" (*American Gigolo*), the theme from *Cat People*, "Flashdance . . . What a Feeling" and "Maniac" (*Flashdance*), "Take My Breath Away" and "Danger Zone" (*Top Gun*), "The Heat Is On" and "Axel F" (*Beverly Hills Cop*), "Shakedown" (*Beverly Hills Cop II*), "How Do I Live" (*Con Air*), "Gangsta's Paradise" (*Dangerous Minds*), and "I Don't Want to Miss a Thing" (*Armageddon*). Additionally, several of his films have profoundly affected fashion, most notably *American Gigolo*, for its sanctification of Armani; *Flashdance*, for its exaltation of exposed-shoulder distressed sweatshirts; and *Top Gun*, for igniting the skyrocketing sales of Ray-Ban Aviator sunglasses and bomber jackets . . . not to mention *Pirates of the Caribbean* and the advent of Captain Jack Sparrow outfits.

BEGINNINGS

For Bruckheimer, the road less traveled began in Detroit, Michigan, where he was the only child born to lower middle-class, German-Jewish immigrant parents. His father, Ludwig, was a clothing salesman, and his mother, Anna, was a bookkeeper and housewife, whose remarkable longevity allowed her to enjoy her son's success until she passed away in 2009 just shy of her 104th birthday. A good deal of Jerry Bruckheimer's love of country can be traced to the appreciation his parents had for the United States. America opened its arms to them and allowed them the opportunity to not only survive, but, to a modest degree, succeed. "They were lucky to get out of Germany when they did," notes Bruckheimer, "because several of their relatives didn't survive Hitler." Although Ludwig and Anna spoke German at home "when they didn't want me to understand what they were saying," Bruckheimer points out that his parents chose not to teach him the language because they were concerned that he might develop a German accent as he was growing up in the postwar years.

Very little in Jerry Bruckheimer's childhood would hint at what was to come later in life. He grew up in a house so small that, "I could stretch out my arms in my bedroom and touch both walls." Hollywood must have seemed as if it were a million miles away from Michigan.

Through television and visits to the local movie theaters in Detroit, young Jerry Bruckheimer discovered and devoured the kinds of films boys around the world have always enjoyed—those loaded with action and a high entertainment quotient, whether they were John Ford Westerns; Cecil B. DeMille biblical spectacles; or, later in life, the muscular, no-nonsense action of John Sturges's *The Great Escape*; and, especially, the epic visions of David Lean in *The Bridge on the River Kwai* and *Lawrence of Arabia* (the latter often cited by Bruckheimer as his all-time favorite film). Bruckheimer found pleasure in the tried-and-true formulas of genre movies. "I used to go to every possible matinee," recalls the producer, "dreaming

of working in the movies someday." What the youthful Bruckheimer found at the movies was his very calling in life; but at that point, it was an impossible dream.

"All I ever wanted to do was make movies," Bruckheimer recalled in a June 2009 address to a commencement class at Centre College in Kentucky. "Not unlike thousands of other young people all across the world. Not having any connections, not living anywhere near the action, and having no financial means to get me there, it was a far-fetched fantasy. While I was concerned about getting out of Detroit, my parents were concerned about getting me out of twelfth grade. But I had a dream, and I was determined to see it through, even if that meant I had to somehow graduate from high school."

During those high school years, Bruckheimer did find a way to be close to film. Having avidly taken up photography at the age of six, after his uncle gave him an old camera, he continued taking photos. By the time he was in the tenth grade, he had begun printing his own work and entering

ABOVE AND RIGHT:
A very young Jerry Bruckheimer with his warm and strong-spirited mother, Anna, who proudly lived to see him rise to the very top of the motion picture and television industries.

some of it in competitive photo shows. He ultimately became a good enough young photographer to garner an Honor Award from the Eastman Kodak Company "for distinguished achievement in amateur photography as selected by the National Board of Judges of the 1959 Kodak High School Photo Contest." He recalls, "From the time my uncle gave me that first camera, I saw things that I wanted to record on film. And when I won some awards, that encouraged me to continue doing it. [I] always loved taking pictures, and I'm still carrying the camera around."

But he also enjoyed other classic boyhood pursuits, supplementing his love of movies with a passion for ice hockey (both as a spectator and amateur player) that continues to this day, as well as a love of cars—another interest that has never left him. Bruckheimer discovered an early proclivity for leadership and organization, putting together pickup baseball and hockey teams (he is still doing the latter on a weekly basis) and making his otherwise quiet home a meeting place for neighborhood friends—although those skills didn't necessarily translate into strong grades.

After graduating Mumford High School in Detroit as "a solid C student," Bruckheimer alighted for the warm climes of Arizona, beginning his college studies with a year at Arizona State University, before transferring to the University of Arizona, where he studied and received a liberal arts bachelor's degree.

The classic Horatio Alger, Jr. thrust of Jerry Bruckheimer's story really began after college graduation in 1965, when he entered the world of advertising. He was hired "beneath the ground floor" at the age of twenty-one by the firm MacManus John & Adams in Bloomfield Hills, near his native Detroit. His parents, Ludwig and Anna, "were disappointed that I didn't become a doctor, lawyer, or dentist." At the agency, Bruckheimer quickly discovered

that those who put in the most effort were the ones who began rising quickly. He volunteered for every opportunity to take on extra tasks, and soon worked his way out of the mail room.

Closely observing the firm's work, Bruckheimer soon learned how to use the sixty-second commercial format to tell ministories, and sell the product at the same time. "You have to be very precise in telling that story in such a short amount of time," says Bruckheimer, "and you learn pretty quickly that you have to make what you're selling very clear to the public." One of his earlier successes was a parody that cleverly utilized Arthur Penn's sensational 1967 gangster film *Bonnie and Clyde* to sell Pontiac automobiles. It was cited for its brilliance by *Time* magazine and brought Bruckheimer to the attention of BBDO, a colossus in the world of advertising.

Ironically, for a man who would be a future jet-setter by sheer necessity, Jerry Bruckheimer stepped onto an airplane for the very first time at the age of twenty-three, setting off to the East Coast and the next step in his career. At BBDO, the wonder boy was soon assigned prime campaigns, winning several CLIO Awards in the process. There's no doubt that he could have enjoyed a long and lucrative lifetime career as a prisoner of Madison Avenue, but Bruckheimer had another dream: to produce films. Thus, he traded one coast for another after three-and-a-half years as one of New York's most promising Mad Men, and moved west to Los Angeles in 1970 at the invitation of commercial director Dick Richards, who was about to transition to the big screen. "You always aspire to do something more, and doing thirty- or sixty-second commercials was only part of telling a story. I was enamored with films, and since I didn't go to film school, advertising gave me the means to acquire the knowledge and technical aspects of filmmaking."

Even as a young boy, Jerry Bruckheimer
was never far from a camera.

Ridley Scott, one of the best commercial directors in the industry before his ascension as an even more celebrated feature director, recalled the moment when he learned that Bruckheimer had decided to precede him on that path. "I had a relationship with Jerry Bruckheimer for years," recalled Scott in 2001 during production of *Black Hawk Down*, "but the last time I worked with him was about thirty years ago when I was directing a BFGoodrich tire commercial in San Francisco, and Jerry was the producer for the agency. After we finished, we were driving back to the hotel, and Jerry said, 'You know, this is my last commercial.' I asked him what he was going to do next, and Jerry responded that he wanted to produce movies. And I said, 'Oh, yeah? Sure!'" recollected Scott with a laugh.

But that was exactly what he did. Bruckheimer's first motion-picture credit, in 1972, was as associate producer of the revisionist Western *The Culpepper Cattle Co.*, the first of four films in which he teamed with Dick Richards.

That was forty-one years and forty-seven feature films ago. After that initial affiliation with Richards, Bruckheimer was one of the producers on four films in the early 1980s, three of which had a real impact on the changing aesthetics of the day: Paul Schrader's provocative *American Gigolo* and *Cat People*, and Michael Mann's acclaimed feature directing debut, *Thief*. The sleek, stylish palettes of these films were a definite contrast to the gritty, neorealist tone of the preceding decade's cinematic highlights, such as William Friedkin's *The French Connection* or Sidney Lumet's *Serpico* and *Dog Day Afternoon*.

BIRTH OF A LEGEND

During these formative years of Jerry Bruckheimer's producing career, MTV, a game-changing network, first flickered onto home TV screens and the national consciousness on August 1, 1981. With that launch, the landscape of film and television would never be the same . . . and neither would American and world culture. Now ministories would be told not just in thirty- or sixty-second commercials, but in music videos as well, welcoming a whole new generation of visually driven filmmakers who saw movies not as staged theater, but a medium unto itself. It was during this cinematic evolution that Bruckheimer and a friend—the Alaska-born, hugely energetic former publicist and studio executive Don Simpson—decided to form a producing partnership. The two had met nearly ten years earlier at a screeing of the Jamaican film *The Harder They Come*, and formed a perhaps unlikely friendship.

Although near opposites in character—Simpson, the loquacious and often outrageous extrovert, and Bruckheimer, the quiet, steady hand—the two enjoyed an incredibly fruitful partnership from their initial blockbuster effort, *Flashdance*, through a breathtakingly successful string of hits, which placed them at the very top of the Hollywood power list for more than a decade.

The pair decided to go their separate ways shortly before Simpson's tragic death in January 1996. But one year later, the newly created Jerry Bruckheimer Films enjoyed the first of a seemingly endless run of stunning successes with *Con Air*, reestablishing him as a massive force in entertainment. And the advent of Jerry Bruckheimer Television soon thereafter only widened his arena.

Since that time, Bruckheimer has forever altered the terrain of both feature films and television, and is one of a handful of producers to have wielded such a remarkable degree of creative power and influence. The scope and sensibilities of Bruckheimer's films have grown considerably since the Don Simpson/Jerry Bruckheimer years, revealing the producer's yearning to flex his creative muscles and take chances, often breaking completely free of any hint of high concept, as demonstrated by such offbeat projects as *Pirates of the Caribbean: The Curse of the Black Pearl*, which, despite its now historic status, was a gigantic shot in the dark. While continuing his mainstay of big-budget, high-octane action-adventure films, Bruckheimer has also experimented with genres not generally associated with him, such as romantic comedy (*Confessions of a Shopaholic*) and animation (*G-Force*). Bruckheimer had already demonstrated an interest in smaller, socially relevant dramas with *Dangerous Minds* during the Don Simpson/Jerry Bruckheimer days, and, once he was on his own, he pursued this interest further with *Remember the Titans*, *Veronica Guerin*, and *Glory Road*.

Bruckheimer has enjoyed some of the longest-running professional affiliations in the industry with talent both in front of and behind the camera, including multiple collaborations with actors such as Johnny Depp (five times), Nicolas Cage (seven times), Tom Cruise (two times), Denzel Washington (three times), Will Smith (three times), Gene Hackman (three times), and Jon Voight (five times); directors like Tony Scott, Michael Bay, Jon Turteltaub, Gore Verbinski, and Paul Schrader; and an entire spectrum of behind-the-camera talent, some of whom have worked on more than a dozen Bruckheimer productions over the span of many years.

Many of Bruckheimer's top executives and other employees have been with him for years, displaying a loyalty which is quite rare in an industry that all too often survives on a scorpion-in-a-bucket mentality. Mike Stenson has been with Bruckheimer since 1998, and Chad Oman's been there even longer, since 1995; JBF Executive Vice President Melissa Reid joined in 2000, while postproduction chief Pat Sandston has been on board since 1995, and Director of Development Charles Vignola, the longest runner, has been working for the producer since 1990. In the television division, President Jonathan Littman came to Jerry Bruckheimer Television in 1997, and Executive Vice President KristieAnne Reed, who began as a production coordinator on *Con Air* in 1996, followed that project by joining the company the following year as an executive assistant to Bruckheimer before being promoted to handling executive capacities, first in features, and then in TV. Bruckheimer has also enjoyed long-running affiliations with his agents at Creative Artists Agency, his attorney Jake Bloom (thirty years), accountants, and publicists. In the latter capacity, Paul Bloch of Rogers & Cowan has functioned as the producer's personal press representative for more than twenty-five years.

Ask any of these people the reason for their enduring affiliations with Bruckheimer and the answers will all be similar. "We never have a dull moment, that's for sure," laughs Barry Waldman, whose long history working with Bruckheimer as line producer, handling the huge day-to-day logistics of some of the biggest productions in recent history, dates back to *The Rock* and has included eleven films in all. "We don't set any boundaries for ourselves," he continues. "Jerry is a great visionary, and we really strive to do things that have not been done before. From our standpoint, our job is to turn those script pages into reality, and it makes you set your goals really high. On Jerry Bruckheimer films, we don't take no for an answer."

THE MAN BEHIND THE LIGHTNING BOLT

But there are two Jerry Bruckheimers: the brand, and the man himself. And though obviously closely aligned, they are not necessarily one and the same. Bruckheimer avidly promotes his films by participating in premieres, press junkets, and interviews, but that's his public face, and it's

Jerry and Linda Bruckheimer with daughter Alexandra Balahoutis, when she was still a young girl.

One of Hollywood's most successful partnerships:
Jerry and Linda Bruckheimer.

Jerry Bruckheimer and daughter
Alexandra Balahoutis in Los Angeles.

all about the work. Unlike other high-profile producers, both past and present, Bruckheimer doesn't swing open the doors to his own personal life, wear his heart on his sleeve, or lay out his life history. Like most visual artists, Bruckheimer believes that a picture (or a movie) speaks a thousand words, and prefers to let them do the talking for him. "When I do interviews, I'm not promoting myself," he explains. "I'm promoting what we've done." The man himself is intensely private and enigmatic by reputation, soft-spoken, and unquestionably shy. "When you're Jerry Bruckheimer," offered one acquaintance, "you don't have to speak loudly." He moves quickly, and doesn't engage in a great deal of idle chitchat or small talk. His smile is genuine and warm, even contagious, and his loyalty and generosity to longtime associates, employees, and friends is legendary. But occasionally, the smile functions much as it does in some Eastern cultures, as a mysterious and protective shield.

Bruckheimer's consistent Zen-like calm amazes even those who have worked with him for decades. The man is seemingly incapable of becoming rattled. "I have never once heard Jerry raise his voice to a high decibel," notes Mike Stenson. "It's when he gets even quieter than usual that you have to be concerned."

"My guess would be, he doesn't waste time talking about things, he does things," said Nicolas Cage to *Daily Variety*'s David S. Cohen in July 2006. "Jerry is a doer, and he knows there's great power in silence."

Jerry Bruckheimer's private life is kept just that—private—even, to a great extent, from longtime associates and employees. He has little interest in promoting himself outside of the boundaries of his workplace. However, he does not live a hermetic existence, cut off from the mainstream of human interaction. In striking contrast to the stereotypical "Hollywood relationship," he's been enamored of the same woman for thirty-eight years: his wife, Linda, a former *Mirabella* magazine editor, who later became an acclaimed novelist for her evocative and perceptive tales of Southern life in *The Southern Belles of Honeysuckle Way* and *Dreaming Southern*. Together, they raised Linda's daughter by a previous marriage, Alexandra Balahoutis, a creative entrepreneur in her own right, who is the founder of Strange Invisible Perfumes.

Linda Bruckheimer has proven to be equally as dynamic as her husband in her own creative pursuits, which—in addition to her writing—also include her remarkable work serving on the board of The National Trust for Historic Preservation in Washington, D.C., and as a custodian of her native Kentucky's architectural and cultural heritage. An avid preservationist, Linda Bruckheimer created a living museum on the couple's Kentucky spread, Walnut Groves Farm, which is comprised of an 1820 Greek Revival main house and several lovingly restored historic buildings that otherwise might have fallen prey to demolition (including a cabin which belonged to the great-uncle of one of Kentucky's most heralded native sons, Abraham Lincoln). Linda also, by sheer force of will, spearheaded the restoration and renovation of downtown Bloomfield, the nearest community to the farm, and now a showpiece of Main Street Americana. The centerpieces of downtown are the Olde Bloomfield Meeting Hall, with four lanes of bowling, pool tables, and a wood-floored roller rink (open to families on Friday and Saturday nights), and Nettie Jarvis Antiques, a quaint shop on Taylorsville Road that was named for Linda's great-grandmother.

Almost every fall, the Bruckheimers host a company retreat at Walnut Groves, in which Linda's talents as a producer in her own right truly come to light in a nonstop cavalcade of dazzling events

and contests. An all-day meeting that kicks off the retreat inevitably ends with Bruckheimer's softly spoken, but pointed battle cry: "Let's go get 'em!"

While fully supporting his wife's endeavors, Jerry has several of his own, including his long-standing passion for sports in general, and ice hockey in particular, that led him to create weekly pickup games with teams comprised of professional players and enthusiastic amateurs, some of them actors and filmmakers. Each year, Bruckheimer hosts the Bad Boys Hockey Tournament in Las Vegas, sort of a private Stanley Cup for pure fun and exercise. Bruckheimer also loves animals, particularly dogs, and any one of a number of his beautiful golden retrievers can be found in the Jerry Bruckheimer Films and Television office on any given day, keeping him and all of the employees company . . . except when they stare wistfully during a lunch break, silently begging for goodies. More canines populate the Bruckheimers' homes, along with some cats as well, a few of which have been adopted.

Not unexpectedly, when time allows, the Bruckheimers enjoy a night out at the movies, which means going to their local theater along with other paying customers. "We like going to the movies the way everybody else does," he notes, "with a box of popcorn and a big crowd, not in an industry screening room. It's a communal, shared experience, which is why theatrical film exhibition will never be totally replaced by watching movies at home, no matter how big the TV may be."

Considering Bruckheimer's workload, vacations aren't much of an option. "I don't really take many of them," he admits. "When I was young, my father told me not to choose a line of work in which you can't wait for a vacation. When you really love what you do, you don't really feel the need to get away." But for some form of relaxation, he

loves to photograph with a battery of high-tech cameras, often on the sets of his own films, and some of those incisive images have even been displayed in exhibitions around the world. Indeed, a British makeup artist on the *Prince of Persia* set in Morocco innocently asked one day in the desert, "Who's the new unit photographer?" not realizing that it was actually Jerry Bruckheimer himself. Often, until the producer positions himself in a chair with his name on it next to the director in a "video village" (where the filmmakers sit in front of a cluster of small TV monitors that allow them to see what the camera is pointed at), his low-key presence can go unnoticed.

At the helm of the company, though, Bruckheimer has his finger on every switch of every project, with no detail too small not to be scrutinized. From pre- to postproduction, and the shooting in between, the producer is deeply involved in all creative aspects of the film. "When we were editing *Remember the Titans*, after seeing the film for the first time, Jerry started giving the director incredibly precise notes off the top of his head," recalls Chad Oman. "He was changing the order of specific shots within scenes, as well as moving whole scenes around to restructure the story."

Says Mike Stenson, "Jerry is like a great NBA coach. He puts an all-star team together, pushes for the best from everybody, and calls the plays. Jerry tends to be more hands-on than most producers, which is why, when you look at his body of work, there is a certain sensibility to it all."

To Jerry Bruckheimer Films director of development Charlie Vignola, who has now worked for Bruckheimer since the Don Simpson/Jerry Bruckheimer days, the through-line of the producer's work is "the working-class guy or girl who succeeds against all odds and makes good. You see this in so many of Jerry's films, from Alex Owens in *Flashdance* and Axel Foley in *Beverly Hills Cop*, all the way to Captain Jack Sparrow in the Pirates of the Caribbean films, Rebecca Bloomwood in *Confessions of a Shopaholic*, and Dastan in *Prince of Persia*. Perhaps it's a reflection of Jerry's own humble beginnings, and his incredible success in a very tough business."

Although Bruckheimer is indeed highly collaborative, he also runs his company with a strong personal imprint, a "buck stops here" philosophy, and methods that recall the Hollywood of the past, including the hiring of multiple screenwriters for each project. "Different writers have different strengths," Bruckheimer points out, "which is why in the old days one writer would be assigned by the studio for character, [and] another for dialogue. You can see those divisions on the credits of old movies: 'Teleplay by' so-and-so, 'Dialogue by' so-and-so."

Part of the reason for this strong understanding is the intimacy that he's created with his own company, Jerry Bruckheimer Films and Television. The business is housed in a one-story, unmarked, anonymous, converted warehouse—which from the exterior still looks like one—on what must be one of the least glamorous streets in an industrial section of Santa Monica, California. Enter the building, however, and the visitor is greeted with an elegantly spare and airy interior warmed by wood-beamed ceilings, modern art, a bubbling fountain, and the rippling murmur of employees deeply engaged—for many hours a day—in the fine art of making movies and television shows. There are just enough movie posters, banners, and framed behind-the-scenes stills from projects past and present to indicate that the visitor is in Bruckheimer Central. And if there's any doubt, there's an impossibly realistic life-size figure of Captain Jack Sparrow in the company's kitchen area to remind you. A pool table and espresso bar look inviting, but are only occasionally

used, with work definitely dominating leisure.

There are approximately forty employees, including executives, support staff, and postproduction in a building just across the street from the main headquarters that features editing rooms and a screening room outfitted with all the bells and whistles.

The most prominent features of Jerry Bruckheimer's own office are an imposingly long desk on which an astounding collection of fountain pens are displayed, as well as an exact replica of Captain Jack Sparrow's compass, which was a gift from his wife, Linda; a full-size mannequin wearing the title character's full set of armor from *King Arthur*; a floor-to-ceiling bookcase well stocked with everything from novels to nonfiction, but with a particular emphasis, suitably enough, on film and history; a credenza laden with framed pictures of family, associates, friends, and pets, plus a hockey helmet emblazoned with the famed Pirates of the Caribbean skull logo; and, on the wall, a large chiaroscuro painting of a hockey player that was a gift from his daughter, Alexandra. A big-screen TV (used for watching dailies—the day's work on features and television programs—and promotional materials) is on the opposite wall, as are numerous awards, certificates, binders containing scripts and photos from past films, and more than one letter to Bruckheimer from some of the gentlemen who have inhabited the White House. On a smaller table is the original dice game to which Will Turner (Orlando Bloom) challenged Davy Jones (Bill Nighy) in *Pirates of the Caribbean: Dead Man's Chest*, a gift from director Gore Verbinski.

The typical working day for Jerry Bruckheimer begins at 6:30 a.m.; he wakes up at that hour no matter when he went to sleep the night before. Following a strict fitness regimen (which explains how he maintains a trim and athletic waistline), Bruckheimer works out shortly after

rising, and, notorious multitasker that he is, usually watches episodes of the company's television shows while doing so. Immediately thereafter, the producer eats a light breakfast, then catches up on phone calls, reading, and e-mail before driving to the office, where he spends the day either on the phone or having meetings with staff members, writers, directors, and studio executives. His schedule is rigorously maintained by his indefatigable Chief of Staff Jill Weiss. He often eats at his desk (except for the occasional business lunch), then continues to work until anywhere from 7:00 p.m. to midnight, depending on the workload. More often, Bruckheimer leaves the office at 8:00 or 9:00 p.m. to allow enough time for him to have dinner with his wife, Linda, and catch up on more reading of film and television scripts. He finally turns in at 12:30 a.m. or later, or, when on set during a night shoot, not until sunrise.

Clearly, there's not much time for leisure, nor does Bruckheimer seek it. The emphasis on the importance of rolling up your sleeves and getting hard work done has been a theme throughout Bruckheimer's career, and is central to his personal, nose-to-the-grindstone philosophy. A framed sign hanging in the company's photocopy and supplies room notes, THE WAY YOU DO ANYTHING IS THE WAY YOU DO EVERYTHING. In other words, apply yourself to the small things with the same dedication you bring to the big things. And Bruckheimer constantly emphasizes to aspiring filmmakers and producers that hard work ultimately determines everything: there are no easy tickets to the big time.

Or at least, there shouldn't be.

Because, despite the box office, the honors, the accolades, the almost endless procession of blockbusters on screens large and small, Bruckheimer is the last one to consider resting on his laurels. In fact, he openly admits that he's continually driven by the fear of failure, an astonishing confession from a man who has spent nearly his entire professional life ticking off one success after another. "The ones who pay attention to their failures are the ones who will succeed," he says. "I learn from my mistakes, and I learn from the audience. I don't look back and celebrate. I just always worry about the next one. Do I worry about it? Yes. Do I ever second-guess myself? No."

Jerry Bruckheimer is almost never second-guessed by the actors and filmmakers who have worked with him through the years. "Jerry is sort of the Great Protector," explains Johnny Depp. "He wards off all and any evil spirits. And if anyone had anything really grave at stake in the beginning of Pirates, it was Jerry. Talk about rolling the dice. I mean, for an actor, you come in, do your bit, and if it works it works, and if it doesn't it doesn't, and it's on to the next one. But Jerry really took a risk.

"We wouldn't have been able to get away with a third of what we got away with on the first Pirates without Jerry," Depp continues. "Without his support and his understanding of the material, saying, 'Okay, I know that some people are scared, but this sure seems funny to me, why don't we go with it?' the first film would have been much more generic, not much fun, and I would have been fired! Jerry knows these films well. I've been in umpteen script meetings with the guy, and whenever a false note comes up, he always comes up with something interesting. And if you're in a pinch, he's always the guy who says, 'Don't worry about it. We'll get it taken care of.' Jerry really produces; he's untamed all the time and allows us to be in an atmosphere that's conducive to making something interesting and different. There have never been pressures in that regard. It's always sort of, you know, Bruckheimer's got it. You know he's handling it. It's cool."

Says Nicolas Cage, "Working with Jerry, it's miraculous how it all happens. He creates a spontaneous environment in which you can't help but search into the deepest part of your creative energy to find a solution to every issue. It's like jazz. Everyone starts coming up with ideas at the spur of the moment that are very fresh and electric. On Jerry's movies, you're on a high wire without a net, and every time something good comes out of it. That's what keeps me coming back, and I'd like to think that's what keeps Jerry coming back to me."

Dame Helen Mirren, who starred with Cage in *National Treasure: Book of Secrets*, recalled in her autobiography, *In the Frame,* the disconnect between Bruckheimer's sometimes forbiddingly austere image and the reality: "Jerry Bruckheimer, always dressed in black, but with a nature that contradicted his sartorial choice, was gentle, supportive, and courageous, proving the saying 'he who dares, wins.' . . . Jerry never flinched or shouted or made anyone feel bad. He was shy and reserved, and utterly committed. I loved him."

"We learn from our mistakes," Bruckheimer told that crowd of eager graduating students at Centre College in June 2009. "You might have heard about a convenient technique called 'take two.' Well, in my industry, we have lots of chances to get it right, sometimes dozens and dozens of chances. This might sound like a dream come true, but filmmaking can be a grueling and complex process. A producer needs skills that are both artistic and technical.

"You are part businessman, philosopher, psychologist, and more . . . the end result is a fusion of creativity and blood, sweat, and tears . . . and in the end, a wonderful thing called magic. . . . Excellence demands vigilance; it requires one to constantly push to a higher level. It is achieved when you remain true to your personal vision, when you refuse to

let anyone dampen the fire burning inside. And excellence can never be taken for granted or rest on its laurels.

"There were no shortcuts when I started out, and there aren't any today," the producer concluded. "God has given everybody a gift, and your task is to find yours, develop it, and dream beyond your ability."

Luckily for us, Jerry Bruckheimer has found his gift. And he found it at the movies.

THE CULPEPPER CATTLE CO.

HOLLYWOOD:THE EARLY YEARS

"A lot of people thought I was out of my mind when I left New York. But I always bet on myself, and I always had a lot of faith that I could be as good as I could be. Faith comes from my confidence in myself. I felt I could always go back, but once I left, I never looked back."
– Jerry Bruckheimer to journalist Jane Ammeson, April 2003

Wanting to expand his horizons into feature films, Jerry Bruckheimer left a lucrative job at New York City's biggest advertising agency for an associate producing gig on *The Culpepper Cattle Co.*, a "little tiny Western" for 20th Century Fox that was budgeted at a measly one million dollars.

The Culpepper Cattle Co. (1972) was also the film debut of former commercial director and magazine photographer Dick Richards. "[Bruckheimer] was one of the top advertising producers in New York City," recalled Richards to journalist (and now a film critic with *The New York Times*) Manohla Dargis in 1998, "working for a major agency and making about $100,000 a year, which is equivalent to probably $500,000 a year now. And he took a job as the associate producer for $25,000, just because he loved movies and wanted to make them."

Bruckheimer and Richards would collaborate on four features, and although they made a modest splash in the industry, each one was indicative in some way of what was to come later for the young producer. "I was a new kid in town, an interloper," Bruckheimer recalls, "but we worked our asses off and managed to get the movies done."

The Culpepper Cattle Co. was part of a revisionist Western movement, which flared up in the late '60s and perhaps is best typified by Sam Peckinpah's *Ride the High Country*, *The Wild Bunch*, and *Pat Garrett and Billy the Kid*; Robert Altman's *McCabe and Mrs. Miller*; and Arthur Penn's *Little Big Man*. A Hollywood response not only to the romantic, sanitized image of cowboys and gunfighters propagated in Hollywood since the dawn of movies, but also to the upstart "spaghetti Westerns" emanating from Italy since the early '60s, revisionist Westerns sought to right old wrongs in the perception of life in the Old West.

Now something of a cult film, *The Culpepper Cattle Co.* was a dark coming-of-age story that was strong on sepia-toned imagery—much of which seemed to emerge from old tintypes—and told a classic story of an innocent's harsh education. Playing opposite young lead Gary Grimes (who had made an impressive debut the previous year in *Summer of '42*) as a "Little Mary" (a cook's helper on a cattle drive), the film was blessed with a strong cast of character actors who seemed to have been born in their buckskins, including Billy Green Bush, Luke Askew, Bo Hopkins, Geoffrey Lewis, and Wayne Sutherlin.

Another three years would go by before Richards and Bruckheimer would get another film into release, but in 1975 they had two: the quirky, freewheeling and very '70s road comedy *Rafferty and the Gold Dust Twins*, followed by a period adaptation of Raymond Chandler's *Farewell, My Lovely*. The former was written by John Kaye, who would go on to scribe two other films that flirted with a counterculture still popular

with Hollywood studios: *American Hot Wax* and the Hunter S. Thompson-inspired *Where the Buffalo Roam*. *Rafferty*, on which Bruckheimer again received associate producer credit, starred Alan Arkin as a down-at-the-heels driving instructor who gives a ride to a couple of dubious hitchhikers portrayed by Sally Kellerman and Mackenzie Phillips, who then attempt to kidnap him. Wending its eccentric way through the western U.S., *Rafferty and the Gold Dust Twins* was a film very much of its era, and all the better for it. The film is stamped with a thoroughly rebellious, indie sensibility, but was in fact released by Warner Bros. at a time when big Hollywood studios were taking chances with such films.

Farewell, My Lovely, however, was of another time—the hard-boiled world of Raymond Chandler's 1940s gumshoe Philip Marlowe—and Richards chose to keep true both to the novel and the era, despite the fact that the character had been contemporized in 1969's *Marlowe* and Robert Altman's 1973 *The Long Goodbye*. Among other things, *Farewell, My Lovely* was notable for being Jerry Bruckheimer's first full credit as producer (sharing it with George Pappas).

The film was graced with a fine screenplay by David Zelag Goodman, one of the best writers of his time, with such credits as *Lovers and Other Strangers*, *Monte Walsh*, and Sam Peckinpah's *Straw Dogs*. The gloriously evocative production design was created by Dean Tavoularis, who had recently excelled with Francis Ford Coppola's *The Godfather* and *The Godfather Part II*, winning an Academy Award for the latter. Bruckheimer's education as

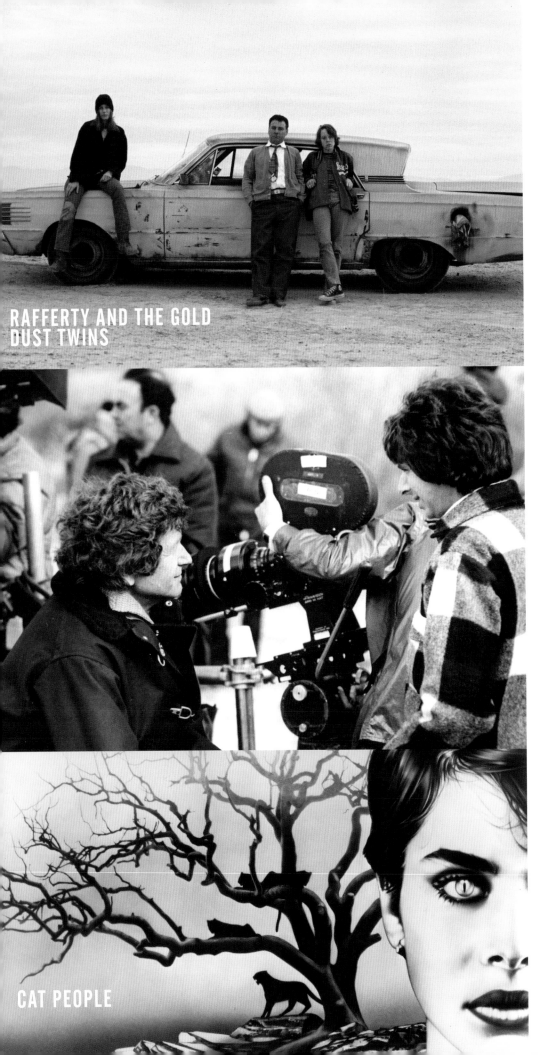

RAFFERTY AND THE GOLD DUST TWINS

CAT PEOPLE

a producer included dealing with the legendary and highly unpredictable Robert Mitchum, who portrayed Marlowe. "Mitchum was a real character who told the greatest stories," recalls Bruckheimer. "Nice guy, but very complicated."

Bruckheimer and Richards's fourth and final filmic collaboration was prescient in the sense that it anticipated the producer's later predilection for stubbornly reviving genres that had long since faded from the scene. *March or Die* (1977) was the first French Foreign Legion film to be shot in English since the 1966 remake of the silent classic *Beau Geste*. Partially filmed on vast desert landscapes in Morocco, *March or Die* was to be Bruckheimer's first foray into epic-style filmmaking, and a *Lawrence of Arabia*-esque nod to his favorite director, David Lean.

March or Die had a strong international cast, including Gene Hackman, Italy's "spaghetti Western" star Terence Hill (aka Mario Girotti), France's Catherine Deneuve, Sweden's Max von Sydow, and Britain's Ian Holm and Jack O'Halloran. On the technical side, the film boasted sweeping cinematography by John Alcott (who had shot Stanley Kubrick's *Barry Lyndon* two years before) and a music score by David Lean's favorite composer, Maurice Jarre (*Lawrence of Arabia, Doctor Zhivago, Ryan's Daughter*). And to its credit, the script by David Zelag Goodman and Richards transcended the genre's often ethnocentric predecessors to explore the complexities and folly of Western adventurism and imperialism, while extolling the bravery and grit of the legionnaires themselves. Hackman's Major Foster is a classically conflicted soldier, carrying out orders despite knowing that some of them may not be the most effective way of dealing with a fiercely committed Muslim insurgency fighting for what they believe is right and true.

AMERICAN GIGOLO: THE FIRST LANDMARK

The producer's next—and first solo—venture would help to consolidate his reputation, win a great deal of media attention, and set stylistic precedents that would inform much of his future work. *American Gigolo* (1980) was the third film directed by one of American film's most provocative screenwriters, Paul Schrader, following *Blue Collar* (1978) and *Hardcore* (1979). Earlier, he had written the iconoclastic classic *Taxi Driver* for Martin Scorsese, in which Schrader's signature studies of sexuality, violence, and spiritual yearning were inevitably intertwined. And they would be again in both *American Gigolo* and the follow-up Schrader/Bruckheimer collaboration, *Cat People*.

Confirming Richard Gere as a major new American star (after the previously cast John Travolta decided not to play the role just two weeks before the start of filming), the movie shrewdly hid its more serious themes of spiritual hunger beneath the hip, stylish, and very effective thriller veneer. *American Gigolo* is one of the very few films in American history to have a male escort as its protagonist, and Gere's Julian Kay is, boldly, a male version of countless female characters through the years that have used their sexuality to support expensive tastes. And just as Travis Bickle seemed to emerge from the filthy, hellish streets of late 1970s New York City in *Taxi Driver*, Julian, by striking contrast, is very much part and parcel of the Los Angeles landscape he inhabits, all gleaming surfaces, cool cars, music (both the Giorgio Moroder score and hit Blondie single "Call Me" were Oscar nominated), and Giorgio Armani clothing. And if clothes make the man, then Bruckheimer and Schrader made Armani, who took off into fashion stardom in the wake of the film's release. *American Gigolo* was actually responsible for changing

MIDDLE LEFT:
Jerry Bruckheimer and his first creative
partner in feature films, director Dick Richards.

the way fashion-conscious men dressed once and forever.

One of *American Gigolo*'s greatest strengths was its now emblematic early '80s look, in good part attributable to Italy's Ferdinando Scarfiotti, one of the most influential designers of his time and best known for his work with Bernardo Bertolucci. "Ferdinando was visual consultant on the film, and he was an absolute genius," recalls Bruckheimer. "Like any great artist, Ferdinando would see things that nobody else could. He was absolutely unique."

Bruckheimer, Schrader, and Scarfiotti were to collaborate once again two years later on another challenging project, but in between, Bruckheimer produced future directing superstar Michael Mann's first theatrical feature, *Thief* (1981), starring James Caan. With its shimmering, rain-slicked nighttime images of Chicago and pulsating score by the German synth-band Tangerine Dream, *Thief* was a representative aesthetic link between the '70s and '80s, and would come to be greatly influential on the look of crime dramas for the next two decades (not the least of which was Mann's own TV series, *Miami Vice*).

Cat People (1982), the second of Bruckheimer and Paul Schrader's collaborations, can now be seen, in retrospect, as a decidedly more erotic precursor of the Twilight books and films, and stands as the only horror film in the producer's body of work (although one of a high artistic order). In Stephenie Meyer's morally restrained, even puritanical opuses, the teen lovers (albeit one of them being a teen for more than a hundred years) have to resist their own raging hormones, with sex equaling death—or at least an eternal vampirical life/death. This contemporary twist on the 1942 Jacques Tourneur classic was a carnal tale of forbidden love, starring the exotic and alluring Nastassia Kinski in the heart of her career. With a haunting score by Giorgio Moroder—highlighted by David Bowie's theme song—and Scarfiotti's gauzily sensual designs, *Cat People* dwelled in the realm of the mythological rather than

the realistic. The film was an examination, and a convincing one, of the pure animal living inside each human. And, like *American Gigolo*, it seems improbable if not impossible for the film to be bankrolled today by a major studio.

Bruckheimer's other and less well-known productions during his early period were the revenge drama *Defiance* (1980), which has managed to win admirers through the years for its grit and the direction of John Flynn, following his earlier vengeance-driven effort, *Rolling Thunder* (1977), and, somewhat uncharacteristically, Garry Marshall's soap opera spoof, *Young Doctors in Love* (1982).

With all of these early films, Bruckheimer was clearly developing his own aesthetic, absorbing everything he could about filmmaking, and looking forward to the next stage of his career. "All of those films taught me so much about the business, and helped me clarify in my own mind what I wanted to do next." In fact, it was a chance meeting in 1972, which would bring Jerry Bruckheimer into the next phase of his career, one that would change the very air that Hollywood was breathing.

DEFIANCE

THIEF

YOUNG DOCTORS IN LOVE

AMERICAN GIGOLO

HOLLYWOOD HIT MEN
DON SIMPSON / JERRY BRUCKHEIMER PRODUCTIONS

"Our movies are representative of the way we feel. It's our way of trying to rearrange reality. Our movies are representative of the way we'd like to see life go. It'd be nice if life could go like our movies. It doesn't, it can't, but at least for two hours it can."
—Jerry Bruckheimer to UCLA journalist Ben Schwartz, June 29, 1987

"If nothing else is communicated to your readers through this interview, it should be that the way to make movies is with your gut, your heart. All the theories go out the window. Theories don't make movies, hearts do." —Don Simpson to UCLA journalist Ben Schwartz, June 29, 1987

One of Hollywood's most legendary producing partnerships began when Jerry Bruckheimer and Don Simpson met at an industry screening of the Jamaican reggae/crime film *The Harder They Come* in 1972. At that point, both men were ambitious, incredibly bright, and neither had yet made his mark in Hollywood; Bruckheimer was a fledgling producer, and Simpson was working in the Warner Bros. publicity department, not even yet a production executive. "We liked each other," Bruckheimer recalled to interviewer Stephen Rebello in 2003. "Liked a lot of the same things in movies. With him I didn't have to talk much, which was a good thing. He was just a very entertaining personality—vivacious, funny, a great storyteller."

Ten years after that first meeting, the two friends were to become producing partners and change the playing field of how movies were developed, cast, shot, edited, scored, marketed, and distributed, and in the process restore considerable power to creative producers after years of marginalization. "The Producer Is King Again" blared the headline of a May 20, 1985, story by David Ansen in *Newsweek*, with a dual photo of Simpson and Bruckheimer at the top of the article. "The old-fashioned, creative producer is back," wrote Ansen, "and he (and sometimes she) is a hot commodity. No mere check-signer, this hands-on new producer models himself on the likes of Selznick and Dore Schary and Alexander Korda and Sam Spiegel, producers who put their imprint on a movie, producers whose names often surpassed the directors they hired and fired."

Don Simpson, a brash, brilliant native of Alaska with a huge appetite for life, was the complete behavioral opposite of Bruckheimer, the high-decibel yin to Bruckheimer's quieter yang. ("We're like different parts of the same brain," Bruckheimer would say in the mid-'80s, explaining their unexpected synergy, with Simpson adding, "I'm verbal, I'm abstract, Jerry is linear and mathematical.") Working from a long, shared desk with only a small divider between them in their supersleek office on the Paramount back lot, Simpson and Bruckheimer would become famously known, respectively, as "Mr. Inside and Mr. Outside," bookends who complemented each other both personally and professionally.

"They were very different people," recalls Bruckheimer's longtime publicist Paul Bloch, who began his association with the producer during the Simpson/Bruckheimer days, "but they respected and loved each other. I would call Jerry with an idea and he'd tell me to call Don and get his take on it, or I'd call Don first and he would say the same thing about Jerry. They were a true partnership and made decisions together."

"Jerry and Don were larger-than-life characters who bestrode Hollywood when there were only a handful of people who demanded that level of respect, and achieved that level of success," notes Charlie Vignola, whose twenty years of working for Bruckheimer dates back to the partnership era. "They worked very well as a team, and when it came time

OPPOSITE PAGE:
Five movie legends (left to right): director Tony Scott, Don Simpson, screenwriter Robert Towne, Jerry Bruckheimer, and Tom Cruise on the racetrack set of Days of Thunder.

to do business, nobody did it better than Don and Jerry."

Film editor Chris Lebenzon, who worked for the producing team on *Top Gun*, *Beverly Hills Cop II*, *Days of Thunder*, and *Crimson Tide* (and later for Bruckheimer on *Con Air*, *Armageddon*, and *Pearl Harbor*) recalls the unusual attention that Simpson and Bruckheimer paid to every aspect of filmmaking. "They'd always come in together, every day, to check the progress of the editing, and I had never seen that before with producers. They were almost always aligned in their views, were very vocal about what they were seeing, and asked a lot of good questions. They would stay right on top of the movie from day one."

Lebenzon recalls that the team was always focused squarely on the work. "Jerry and Don wouldn't socialize a lot. At around seven o'clock, when other producers around town would have dinner, Jerry and Don were still hard at work, reading scripts or magazines for ideas . . . which is how *Top Gun* wound up getting made. They were the hardest workers in Hollywood."

"We like pictures about triumph," confirmed Simpson to *Life* magazine reporter Margot Dougherty in an April 1987 interview about the high-flying team.

"It parallels our own lives," Bruckheimer added. "We both come from the heartland of America. We worked hard to get here."

"I'm a boy from Alaska," Simpson concluded; "he's a boy from Detroit. We're from lower-middle-class backgrounds, and lo and behold we found ourselves in Hollywood. If we can do it, anybody can."

"I'm not a person who loses control," Bruckheimer would note in retrospect years later, "where Don would just dive right in. He was pedal to the metal, while I was more conscious of what I was doing. It was the tortoise and the hare, really. He was buzzing around, while I took my time

getting where I wanted to go."

Simpson, like Bruckheimer, began his career in advertising, and was then recruited in 1971 by Warner Bros. as a marketing specialist to the then-burgeoning youth market, promoting the likes of counterculture favorites *Woodstock*, *A Clockwork Orange*, *Performance*, *Mean Streets*, and *Billy Jack*. Four years later, Simpson joined Paramount Pictures as a production executive, ultimately rising to the rank of president of worldwide production in 1981. During that tenure, Bruckheimer and Simpson worked together on *American Gigolo*, and, finding common ground, teamed up when circumstances found Simpson leaving that position in 1982.

Bruckheimer explained his synergistic relationship with Simpson to *Fade In* magazine: "[Don] was so smart, and he had knowledge that I didn't have. I didn't understand the

"Hollywood's Hit Men." Don Simpson and Jerry Bruckheimer, outside of their Paramount Pictures office (left), and striking a more casual pose (right).

OPPOSITE PAGE:
Don Simpson and Jerry Bruckheimer on the set of Bad Boys.

system. He was the system. He could walk into any meeting and know what the agenda was, what they were thinking, 'cause he was them. And he developed 120 projects a year. If I'd developed five or six, that was a lot. And he didn't know how to make movies. He didn't have a clue. I had that expertise."

FLASHDANCE: AUSPICIOUS BEGINNINGS

The formation of Don Simpson/Jerry Bruckheimer Productions was announced in *Daily Variety* on August 3, 1983. The duo had been signed to an exclusive three-year deal by Jeffrey Katzenberg of Paramount to develop and produce films. Their initial foray would be a classic story jazzed up with a totally contemporary rock-video sensibility, *Flashdance* (1983). The film would become a phenomenon, a cultural touchstone combining the cultural streams flowing through America at that time, especially music, dance, and female empowerment.

"We've got popcorn hearts and minds," Simpson would be quoted as saying, and the fact that *Flashdance* ultimately grossed more than $217 million in worldwide box office receipts, at a time before such figures were common, proved that an awful lot of popcorn was being eaten all over America. To helm *Flashdance*, Simpson and Bruckheimer selected Adrian Lyne, a British commercials director whose only previous feature had been *Foxes*, a stylish examination of young and restless girls growing up in Southern California's San Fernando Valley, starring a young Jodie Foster and Cherie Currie, of the seminal punk band the Runaways. Working from a script by Tom Hedley and Joe Eszterhas,

with additional contributions by Katherine Reback, *Flashdance* was the first film created for the infant MTV generation, then just two years old. The film's pounding sound track and hook-filled songs underscored the story of Alexandra (Alex) Owens (Jennifer Beals), a working-class, steel-mill welder by day, who moonlights as a provocative dancer at Mawby's Bar, all the while dreaming of studying at the Pittsburgh Conservatory of Dance and Repertory.

Upon the film's release on April 15, 1983, audiences spoke, and loudly, with lines around the block and multiple viewings. The sound track album, an instant pop classic, sold out in the first weekend. Like so many of Bruckheimer's later films, *Flashdance* was plugged right into contemporary culture, not only because of the music, romantic subplot, and Jeffrey Hornaday's almost avant-garde (and now much imitated and satirized) choreography, but because he and Simpson well understood that the better part of the international moviegoing audience was, like Alex, hanging on to their dreams.

"With *Flashdance*," observes Charlie Vignola, "I think Jerry started to set down the paradigm of the working-class hero who has to overcome his or her own demons, both within and without, to basically reach for their dreams and solve their problems. And to do so in ways that are very energetic, dynamic, cinematic, and entertaining. I think it's the protomyth you see in many of Jerry's films, conscious or not. Perhaps because of his own background, Jerry seems to respond to characters who are all-American, not to the manor born; people who have to pick themselves up by the bootstraps. They will fight and not give up until they get the girl, save

the day, solve the problem, or save the world."

Flashdance also gave Don Simpson and Jerry Bruckheimer their first hint at how much their films could influence popular culture, as thousands of young women began imitating Alex Owens's look: the ripped sweatshirt (with exposed shoulder), leg warmers, triple scarves, and fetchingly oversized military jackets that costume designer Michael Kaplan designed for Jennifer Beals. The film also presented a surprisingly powerful vision of untraditional feminism that has been oft-imitated ever since, beginning with the now iconic introduction of Beals's face as she first removes her welding mask and shakes out her full head of curls in a liberating gesture. Alex Owens is a classic tough chick, defensive, protective, and unafraid to slap around her lover, Nick Hurley (Michael Nouri), when she accuses him (unfairly, as it turns out) of cheating on her.

The film instantly established some Don Simpson/Jerry Bruckheimer signatures, including the reliance on evocative imagery rather than just words, to help tell a story written by screenwriters Hedley and Eszterhas. "Adrian Lyne, the director, shot a lot of film," notes Bruckheimer, "but we kept paring away anything that stood in the way of telling Alex's story in a direct way. A lot of scenes wound up on editor Bud Smith's cutting-room floor, but we were trying to invent new ways of getting to the heart of a movie."

Don Simpson/Jerry Bruckheimer's sophomore effort, *Thief of Hearts* (1984), was taken on as a favor to Paramount, as the studio was looking for the producers' expertise to spearhead the project. It was, like *Thief*, another stylish foray into the life of a high-living professional criminal, with

Ferdinando Scarfiotti once again providing his expertise as visual consultant. (From a purely historic perspective, *Thief of Hearts* was notable as the first time Bruckheimer cast David Caruso, eighteen years before the actor began starring in *CSI: Miami*.)

BEVERLY HILLS COP: THE LAUNCHING PAD

It was Don Simpson/Jerry Bruckheimer's next three consecutive productions that truly sanctified the pair and catapulted them to the Hollywood stratosphere. Bookended by the releases of *Beverly Hills Cop* and *Beverly Hills Cop II* (both of which are examined in the Franchise section of this book) was a film that was to consolidate Don Simpson/Jerry Bruckheimer's place in the Hollywood pantheon, and create a superstar. Simpson and Bruckheimer had already been dubbed "Hollywood's Hit Men" in an influential profile on the cover of the *Los Angeles Times* Calendar section on November 18, 1984, just prior to *Beverly Hills Cop*'s opening. Three months later, when *California* magazine posted their "A-list" of "Power in Hollywood" in the March 1985 issue, Don Simpson/Jerry Bruckheimer were right there along with the likes of Dino De Laurentiis, Zanuck/Brown, Ray Stark, David Geffen, and David Puttnam, all titans of that era.

TOP GUN: INTO THE STRATOSPHERE

On March 28, 1985, a story in *Daily Variety* announced that the producers' next project would be a film entitled *Top Gun*, starring twenty-three-year-old Tom Cruise, and directed by Tony Scott, whose only previous feature credit was the provocative vampire film, *The Hunger*. The film was based on a 1983 *California* magazine article by Ehud Yonay entitled "Top Guns" that examined the world of pilots in the elite U.S. Navy TOPGUN program, officially known as the United States Navy Strike Fighter Tactics Instructor (SFTI) program. Bruckheimer read the article and instantly saw a movie in it.

While the world depicted in Yonay's article was obviously fast, exciting, and highly kinetic, there were at least two good reasons not to touch the subject matter with the proverbial ten-foot pole. For one, the U.S. was still reeling from the negative effects of the highly unpopular war in Vietnam, which had only ended in the previous decade, and numerous films about that conflict had cast the military in a dubious light. For another, this kind of "jet pilot" movie had vanished in the late 1950s and not been seen since. "It's true, the genre was totally dead," admits Bruckheimer, "but we decided to come at it from a different angle. It's all about process. It's taking the audience inside a world they know nothing about and showing them how it actually works, and making them a part of all that. That's what *Top Gun* was—we took you into the world of these fighter pilots, how they lived, how they loved, who they were. Before the production, we lived the life. We went to the Officer's Club, we went up in the jets, and we landed in the planes on the carriers. It was wonderful, and we gave the audience the same kind of experience." During filming, Bruckheimer described the film to a *USA Today* journalist as "*Star Wars* on earth."

The right approach for the producers was to jack up the excitement level and appeal to younger audiences with a hip rock-and-roll sensibility, feature a compelling and passionate romance at the story's core, and to cast the hottest young talent in the business in major roles. Although he had already made an impact in a few previous films, most notably Paul Brickman's *Risky Business*, Tom Cruise was to become a superstar with *Top Gun* as Lieutenant Pete "Maverick" Mitchell, who, true to his name, is something of a lone ranger in his F-14 Tomcat jet fighter until he learns that teamwork—and, of course, the love of a good woman—is what makes a real man, and a great pilot.

"I knew that Tom was going to be a movie star," says Bruckheimer. "He had something special. You can see a hundred actors, and all of a sudden, someone will walk into a room and there's a spark. That's something God gave them, or the opportunity presented itself and they were prepared for it." The rest of the *Top Gun* cast was comprised of such younger talents as Kelly McGillis, Val Kilmer, Anthony Edwards, Tim Robbins, Meg Ryan, and Rick Rossovich (most of whom went on to considerable stardom), as well as veterans Tom Skerritt and Michael Ironside. The producing team's unusual selection for director, Tony Scott, marked the beginning of an extraordinary, nearly thirty-year-long personal and professional relationship between the filmmaker and Jerry Bruckheimer, which was to include six vibrantly innovative films, and was only brought to an end by Scott's tragic demise in August 2012. (Two days before he died Scott was doing research with Bruckheimer and Cruise for a *Top Gun* sequel.) Tony Scott brought a fresh eye to an old genre, elegantly examining the behemoths of the sky and the men who pilot them, and effectively depicting the relationship between Maverick and civilian instructor "Charlie" Blackwood (McGillis). And the number-one, chart-topping sound track featured new hits (the Oscar-winning "Take My Breath Away"), old favorites ("You've Lost That Lovin' Feeling"), and, like *Beverly Hills Cop*, another rousing synth-score by German composer Harold Faltermeyer.

With cooperation from Navy brass, *Top Gun* utilized an entire F-14 fighter squadron, with many scenes shot at the actual TOPGUN facilities at Naval Air Station Miramar and the Naval Training Center near San Diego's Lindbergh Field airport. Cruise and the other actors portraying the Top Gun pilots all went through several days of training, and were later actually filmed in the F-14 cockpits (albeit the backseats).

The innovative techniques employed by Scott, Bruckheimer, and Simpson were seen to best advantage in those flying sequences, and the fact that the actors portraying the pilots were all wearing oxygen masks gave the filmmakers an opportunity for much postproduction revision. "The actors never really spoke any dialogue during actual shooting," recalls editor Chris Lebenzon, who cut the film with Billy Weber. "The flying scenes were essentially created in postproduction, when we worked with Tony, Jerry, Don, the writers, and Navy advisers to create the dialogue, which we then recorded."

Although the film would be noted as an ode to good, old-fashioned American patriotism—some, indeed, accused *Top Gun* of being downright jingoistic—the film is actually fairly apolitical. Noted Simpson at the time, very articulately, "Notice it's a nameless, faceless enemy. If we were making a picture that was militaristic or patriotic in its intent, we would have made them Cubans or Russians. . . . We didn't care; it's all a metaphor. We just painted them black—they're like Darth Vader. It doesn't matter who the enemy is, because the intent

of the final scene is that our hero overcomes his fears and succeeds. The enemy is his inner thoughts; that's what he's fighting against. Those black knights in the sky against which he's jousting are merely metaphorical symbols for what's going on inside his own soul." Indeed, *Top Gun* was more interested in honoring the courage, dedication, and precision of the American military man than in proffering any political manifestos.

Once again, a Don Simpson/Jerry Bruckheimer production was to have a huge effect on pop culture, as befits a film that enjoyed a worldwide gross in excess of $353 million following its May 1986 release. The clothing and accoutrements worn by Cruise in the movie spurred an increase in sales of bomber jackets and Ray-Ban Aviator sunglasses. The film broke many home video sales records in a medium that then was still in its relative infancy. Quentin Tarantino performed an entire monologue—written by his *Pulp Fiction* cowriter Roger Avary—devoted to a subversive interpretation of the film's inherent machismo in the independent film *Sleep with Me* (1994). (Coincidentally, Tarantino would make uncredited script-doctor contributions to a couple of Don Simpson/Jerry Bruckheimer films, including *Crimson Tide*. He later wrote the story for and directed a two-part episode of *CSI: Crime Scene Investigation* in 2005.)

And although the critical reception at the time was the usual mixed bag, Paul Attanasio—now a highly regarded screenwriter, but then the film critic for *The Washington Post*—accurately wrote on May 16, 1986, *Top Gun*'s opening day in U.S. cinemas: "Part of Bruckheimer's expertise lies in his ability to cast a movie—not the people on the

screen, but the even more crucial ensemble behind the camera. It is in the alchemy of this process that the characteristic quality of a Don Simpson/Jerry Bruckheimer film—striking visuals, exciting music, straight-ahead narrative drive, and texture around the edges—is created. The essence of Bruckheimer's work in this regard is a precise sense of the nature of filmmaking collaboration—what a director's weaknesses are and how, say, a certain kind of cinematographer might compensate for them—as well as a certain daring in discovering new blood."

"That's part of the thrill we have as filmmakers," says Bruckheimer. "To give people who are talented a chance to show the world they're talented. Because part of our talent is knowing they're talented."

The longevity that *Top Gun* has maintained in the public and critical imagination was demonstrated once again during the summer of 2011. A twenty-fifth-anniversary Blu-ray release resulted in a surprising spate of articles in publications and online debating the film's merits and impact on film and pop culture. And on December 11, 2012, Paramount announced that the film would be rereleased in an exclusive six-day, 3-D engagement in IMAX theaters on February 8, 2013, followed by a Blu-ray and 2-D two-disc set eleven days later. The 3-D conversion—which allowed a new generation to experience the film in a way that audiences in 1986 could not—had been done under the supervision of Tony Scott before his tragic death. Whether one accepted the prevailing and opposing views of the film—that it marked either the death of '70s-style big-studio adventurism, or invented a new form of filmmaking that once and forever broke the medium away from its theatrical roots toward a purely visual experience—*Top Gun* changed American—and global—cinema forever.

The final two Don Simpson/Jerry Bruckheimer films under their deal with Paramount Pictures continued their relationship with director Tony Scott. First, was the smash hit *Beverly Hills Cop II*, which was followed by an ambitious project that they hoped would match *Top Gun*'s success. *Days of Thunder* (1990) was the third collaboration of Don Simpson/Jerry Bruckheimer and Tony Scott, and their second with Tom Cruise, all of them once again feeling the need for speed . . . but this time earthbound on NASCAR racing tracks rather than up in the wild blue yonder. The film was another examination of the impulses that push men to literally drive themselves beyond the safety zone, and into the limits of their endurance, courage, and perhaps foolishness. And once again, the producers and director sought to put the audience in the driver's seat with the same experiential pilot's-seat approach they took with *Top Gun*. Just to make certain to maximize the quality, Bruckheimer and Simpson turned to one of film's most lauded and respected screenwriters, Robert Towne (*The Last Detail*, *Shampoo*, and *Chinatown*—for which he won the Academy Award), who tried to avoid the good 'ol boy clichés of NASCAR.

Days of Thunder fully utilized the star power and charisma of Cruise as hotshot stock car driver Cole Trickle, adding the then virtually unknown young Australian Nicole Kidman to the combustible mix as a brain surgeon with whom he eventually becomes emotionally entangled. (The real-life romance between the two is all too-well chronicled elsewhere.) With strong supporting performances from Robert Duvall, Cary Elwes, Michael Rooker, and Randy Quaid, Scott utilized his considerable skills to re-create the sights and sounds of NASCAR in full booming, basso profundo, Dolby-ized glory. Upon its release in the U.S. on June 27, 1990, the film brought in some $157 million worldwide.

"*Days of Thunder* didn't live up to the expectations the media had for it," Bruckheimer says, "which happens sometimes. That was down to a really rushed postproduction, the shortest we ever had. But it did about $80 million domestic, so it was actually a successful movie for what it cost to make it. I'm really proud of what we accomplished on that film. It was very tough to make, and Tony did a great job handling and balancing both the drama and the action."

THE DISNEY ERA

With their deal at Paramount coming to a close, Don Simpson/Jerry Bruckheimer rejoined their old colleagues from that studio, Michael Eisner and Jeffrey Katzenberg, by entering into a nonexclusive arrangement with Walt Disney Studios. The new pact was announced in the trade publications on January 18, 1991, and began the second chapter of the Don Simpson/Jerry Bruckheimer story, one that would see the pair reaching the highest levels of accomplishment—and ending in heartbreaking tragedy.

After a period of adjustment and development, as well as an industry strike during which business slowed considerably, their first project for Disney was a modestly scaled and budgeted black comedy for the studio's Touchstone Pictures entitled *The Ref* (1994)—a film about a thief (Denis Leary) who winds up mediating between the squabbling couple (played by Judy Davis and Kevin Spacey) whose house he's burglarizing. Directed by the late Ted Demme, *The Ref* was clearly an offbeat choice for the producers, but it was also clear that they were looking to extend their imprint beyond the signature Don Simpson/Jerry Bruckheimer action-adventure spectacles. "We read the script for *The Ref* and knew we could help out with it," notes Bruckheimer. "One of the things that is especially funny about it is that the family in the story is falling apart—and is probably very typical of many families. There is the husband and wife, who are arguing all of the time and on the verge of divorce, a child who is about to be inducted into the junior Mafia hall of fame, and a domineering mother-in-law who is a caricature of all the bad mothers too many people have.

"Don provided extensive notes on the script," he continues, "and we worked with the screenwriters, Ted Demme, and Denis Leary to take it in a more realistic and logical direction. We certainly didn't pull any of the humor, but we did help make the characters a little more grounded in reality."

Eighteen years after *The Ref*'s modest release, the film's semi-cult reputation was cemented when it landed on the list of *Entertainment Weekly* magazine's "The 50 Best Movies You've Never Seen." The article noted, ". . . Ted Demme's twisted and hysterical film . . . is one of the very best anti-Christmas movies."

Bruckheimer and Simpson returned to the action-comedy template in their next effort, this time for Columbia Pictures, bringing the same madcap overlay that turned the first two Beverly Hills Cop movies into such smash hits to a new franchise: *Bad Boys*. Starring Will Smith and Martin Lawrence, *Bad Boys* introduced a young commercials and music video director named Michael Bay to feature films. It would become Bruckheimer/Simpson's second successful franchise (see more on this film in the Franchise section).

The next notch on the Don Simpson/Jerry Bruckheimer belt was the beautifully made *Crimson Tide* (1995), produced for Disney's Hollywood Pictures division, which reunited the team with Tony Scott. In this tense thriller, the real fireworks and suspense are in the dynamics between the two leading actors, set against the claustrophobic backdrop of a U.S. nuclear submarine. As the sub's commanding officer, Captain Frank Ramsey, one of America's most consummate veteran actors, Gene Hackman, enjoyed one of the best roles in his considerable career. And a perfect counterbalance was then relative newcomer Denzel Washington, cast as Lieutenant Commander Ron Hunter, with whom Ramsey clashes when they receive an order to launch missiles on a Russian nuclear installation after an ultranationalist leader seizes power and threatens the United States and its allies.

Crimson Tide was the first Don Simpson/Jerry Bruckheimer film to finally win some real plaudits from the critics. Typical of the response was Roger Ebert's précis in the *Chicago Sun-Times*: "Oddly enough, *Crimson Tide* develops into an actors' picture, not just an action movie. There are a lot of special effects, high-tech gadgets, and violent standoffs, yes, but the movie is really a battle between two wills."

Audiences were as enthusiastic as the critics, with the film exceeding *Bad Boys*' international revenues and making $157 million at the box office.

Clearly, Don Simpson/Jerry Bruckheimer

Productions wasn't just in the action business anymore, which they proved even further in their next film, *Dangerous Minds*, again for Disney's Hollywood Pictures. This inner-city drama of a schoolteacher trying to break through to tough, resistant pupils was the first of Bruckheimer's forays into films that examined the sociopolitical realities of a racially stratified American society (to be followed by *Remember the Titans* and *Glory Road*). Although *Dangerous Minds* (1995) had plenty of cinematic antecedents, from *The Blackboard Jungle* and *To Sir, with Love*, all the way to *Lean on Me* and *Stand and Deliver*, what made the film stand apart was the fact that its protagonist was a woman. "I wanted to do something that wasn't a big-event movie like the others," recalls Bruckheimer, "[but] a film about our educational system. I also wanted to make a film about a hero whose weapon was her mind and imagination, rather than guns and physical strength."

The film was based upon LouAnne Johnson's autobiography, *My Posse Don't Do Homework*, in which she recounted her trials and triumphs teaching African American and Hispanic teens at a tough high school in northern California. Just as they hired Robert Towne to lend heft to *Days of Thunder*, Bruckheimer and Simpson selected another Academy Award-winning screenwriter, Ron Bass (*Rain Man*), to adapt Johnson's book, with later contributions by the famed writer and performer Elaine May. Three-time Oscar nominee Michelle Pfeiffer was cast by Bruckheimer, Simpson, and Canadian director John N. Smith to portray Johnson, one in a series of strong female leading characters in the producers' films.

Simpson and Bruckheimer were drawn to the

inherent value of telling a story about a teacher fighting a lonely battle against an inherently ineffective system. "Our schools are underfinanced and understaffed, and as a result we are losing a generation of kids," said Bruckheimer at the time of filming. "Don and I would like to make teachers heroes again. We wanted to show their struggle with the system, with the kids, and with the environment in which the kids grow up—which many times is their biggest deterrent—and demonstrate that these teachers really are significant role models."

With its greatly successful sound track—comprised of the Grammy Award-winning song "Gangsta's Paradise," and music by Wendy Melvoin and Lisa Coleman—*Dangerous Minds* was not just about youths, but also spoke directly to them. And almost incredibly, perhaps because of the youth connection, *Dangerous Minds* surpassed even *Crimson Tide* by amassing nearly $180 million at the international box office.

A ROCK-SOLID SMASH HIT

But Bruckheimer, knowing that adventure films were an important element of his stock-in-trade, next turned his attention to *The Rock* (1996), also for Disney's Hollywood Pictures. The title refers to Alcatraz, the most famous and notorious prison in American history. The story neatly utilized the now-shuttered facility for a suitably high-testosterone film about a disgruntled detachment of rogue Marines, under Brigadier General Francis Hummel, who take over the once active jail. After taking hostages, the Marines threaten San Francisco with imminent destruction by rockets tricked out with chemical weapons, unless their demands are met for the government to pay reparations to the families of Marines who died on clandestine operations.

The script by David Weisberg, Douglas Cook, and Mark Rosner was solidified with an uncredited rewrite by Aaron Sorkin, already a major presence with his screenplays for *A Few Good Men* and *The American President.*

For the second time in their partnership, Don Simpson and Jerry Bruckheimer called upon Michael Bay, whose dynamic approach to the medium was perfectly matched with the subject matter. Together they enlisted a completely unexpected trio of actors—Sean Connery, Nicolas Cage, and Ed Harris—to portray, respectively, Mason, Goodspeed, and Hummel. All three had tremendous acting chops, but had come from three very different arenas of filmmaking. Connery, who of course was the original Agent 007, was then already in his sixties, and seemed to be inexorably backing up into a well-deserved retreat from moviemaking. Cage, who won a Best Actor Academy Award during the filming of *The Rock* for his devastating portrayal of a doomed alcoholic in *Leaving Las Vegas*, had specialized in offbeat and off-kilter characters in such indies as *Wild at Heart*, *Vampire's Kiss*, and *Raising Arizona*, with occasional forays into studio-based romantic comedy (*Moonstruck*, *Honeymoon in Vegas*, *It Could Happen to You*). Harris was a hugely admired character actor on stage and screen, best known for *The Right Stuff*, *Sweet Dreams*, and *The Abyss*. Together, the combination would be absolutely combustible. And although it was to be Bruckheimer's only film with the now-retired Connery, *The Rock* would be the first of seven

(to this date) fruitful collaborations with Cage.

The Rock not only proved that Connery maintained one of the strongest presences on film, but also utilized Cage's knuckleball deliveries beautifully. This time, plenty of critics applauded the results, agreeing with *Time* magazine's Richard Corliss that the film was, ". . . the team-spirit action movie *Mission: Impossible* should have been. . . . It all works very smartly. The Don Simpson/Jerry Bruckheimer production duo run clever variations on their macho obsessions. . . . Connery and Cage are fine odd-couple buddies—the grizzled lifer and the computer nerd. . . ."

Audiences around the world certainly shared Corliss's enthusiasm, with the film grossing $134 million in the U.S. and more than $200 million overseas, the seventh biggest film of that year.

But Don Simpson would not live to enjoy yet another huge success. With his friend and partner slipping more deeply into addictive behavior, Bruckheimer told an understanding Simpson in the late summer of 1995 about his decision to separate professionally, thinking that he "had to do something to shake him up and into some recognition of his problems." News of the split wasn't announced until it ran in the trade publications in December. On the morning of January 19, 1996, Bruckheimer received a call on the San Francisco location of *The Rock* telling him that Simpson had died in Los Angeles. Perhaps following William Blake's dictum that "the road of excess leads to the palace of wisdom," Simpson had finally lived too large of a life for his heart to sustain, and it had merely stopped, despite the attempts of Bruckheimer and others who loved him to help.

"I had a partner for thirteen years, and a friend

longer than that," says Bruckheimer, "and suddenly he was gone, and I was on my own. It was difficult." Although Bruckheimer keeps most of his personal feelings to himself, he opened up on the matter to journalist Stephen Rebello. "It's like losing a brother," he said of Simpson's death. "Time heals a lot. He'll never get old. He'll always be what he was then. Whatever his last picture was, that's how he'll always be remembered. Many people warned Don about where he was going. I talked with doctors and told him that when this was over, when he got his life back together, we could talk about getting back together. Doctors say that's the best thing you can do. But all of us feel we can live forever. He didn't think he was going to die. I felt I did what I could do."

For Jerry Bruckheimer, the loss of Simpson was emotionally devastating, but the legacy the two shared would hardly be honored by his walking away from the business he had loved and created.

FLASHDANCE

Director Tony Scott with Tom Cruise on the set of Top Gun.

On the Days of Thunder *set, director Tony Scott confers with Tom Cruise.*

THE REF

CRIMSON TIDE

ZZBRA · · · · · · · · · · · · EMERGE
ACTION
MESSAGE

ROM: NATIONAL MILITARY CO
CENTER

Director Tony Scott at the helm of Crimson Tide.

TOP RIGHT:
Jerry Bruckheimer chats with Michelle Pfeiffer
between takes on the set of Dangerous Minds.

RIGHT:
Director Michael Bay directs
one of his many smash hits, The Rock.

BOTTOM MIDDLE:
Nicolas Cage and Jerry Bruckheimer share a
light moment on the set of The Rock.

JERRY BRUCKHEIMER FILMS:
THE TRANSPORTATION BUSINESS

"There's a saying we've said since the beginning. We're in the transportation business. We transport you. Whatever bills have to be paid—putting the kids through college, whatever—you just sit there . . . and get consumed. And you walk out, and hopefully we've moved you somehow; we've made you laugh, made you cry."
—Jerry Bruckheimer to journalist Todd S. Purdum, May 20, 2001

"I had to jump right back in after Don died," says Jerry Bruckheimer, "and keep going. There's nothing else you can do, unless you decide to just throw up your hands. When Don died, I wanted to be more productive."

"Don's passing was hard for Jerry with respect that the friendship and partnership were so important to him," observes Paul Bloch. "Aside from Linda, Don was Jerry's best friend. But we all knew how sharp and dynamic Jerry was, and he hit the road running. The fact that he became so successful on his own was no surprise."

Don Simpson/Jerry Bruckheimer Productions was gone. But Jerry Bruckheimer Films was born almost immediately thereafter, giving life to the now-famous lightning bolt logo

that opens all of its film and television productions. Incidentally, the tree in that logo was modeled on a three-hundred-year-old oak on the Bruckheimers' property in Kentucky.

Jerry Bruckheimer Films started its new life with an immediate winner right out of the chute: *Con Air* (1997), for Disney's Touchstone Pictures. *Con Air* is now famous for being the film that confirmed Nicolas Cage's status as a full-fledged action star, the actor seemingly reborn as a startlingly muscular, even dangerous, soul who's not to be messed with.

Directed by Simon West, another find who emerged from the world of advertising and commercials to make his debut as a feature filmmaker, *Con Air* is a quintessential Bruckheimer action film. "When the audience sees the lightning logo," the producer joked at the time, "they know they're going to be assaulted." But in addition to the strong performances by Cage, John Malkovich (another case of brilliant casting against type), John Cusack, and the character-rich bevy of supporting players, *Con Air* also had lashings of humor along with the pumped-up action. "I pushed for *Con Air* to be more character-oriented than it was initially," the producer said at the time of production. "Each character is rich in dimension and

interesting, although not necessarily on the right side of the law. This is what ultimately attracted our incredible cast, actors not usually associated with action-adventure films. I believe *Con Air* transcends the conventional action genre, and I hope it will set a new standard for the action genre of the nineties."

It was eminently clear upon the film's initial screenings that the producer had retained everything in the formula that had made his and Simpson's films successes, while adding the dimension of character that Bruckheimer had always championed. Wrote Todd McCarthy in *Variety*: "Hiply written and cast . . . this first official solo effort by producer Jerry Bruckheimer is as surefire commercial, and just as elaborate, as anything he did with his late partner, Don Simpson."

Once again, the audience responded enthusiastically. A $100-million-plus domestic gross was surpassed by the international take of $122 million, bringing *Con Air*'s worldwide total to $224 million.

ARMAGEDDON: HOLDING BACK THE APOCALYPSE

Con Air was a very auspicious beginning for Jerry

Bruckheimer Films, as borne out by the company's next production, the blockbuster science fiction adventure *Armageddon*. Catapulting director Michael Bay to superstar ranking (he was also a producer on the film with Bruckheimer and Gale Anne Hurd), *Armageddon* would become the single biggest worldwide hit of 1998 with a total take of more than half a billion dollars. It took the sometimes dubious genre known as the "disaster film" to new heights with a very healthy budget, state-of-the-art visual effects, and the kind of blast-the-audience-through-the-back-of-their-seats intensity that Jerry Bruckheimer's name had become associated with. In other words, more bang for the audience's buck. With a screenplay by Jonathan Hensleigh and J. J. Abrams, with Tony Gilroy and Shane Salerno adding their own contributions, the story was a canny combination of end-of-the-world scenarios combined with science fiction, and a considerable amount of science fact as well, with classic Bruckheimer working-class heroes led by Harry Stamper (Bruce Willis), the world's foremost deep-core oil driller. Stamper and his team of roughnecks are enlisted by NASA executive director Dan Truman (Billy Bob Thornton) to land on, and then destroy, an asteroid the size of Texas that is heading at 22,000 miles per hour on a collision course with Earth.

"I love stories that are bigger than life," said Bruckheimer during production of the release from Disney's Touchstone Pictures, "especially when the plot is multilayered, as this one is. *Armageddon* isn't just about an asteroid heading for Earth with the potential to destroy it. It's really a story about individuals who are faced with life-and-death decisions. It's also about characters—something akin to *The Dirty Dozen* in outer space."

A late-in-the-day addition to *Armageddon* that would ultimately become one of the film's signature moments well illustrates Bruckheimer's relentless pursuit of making what's already good all the more spectacular. "Jerry and Michael Bay went to the Cannes Film Festival and showed about twenty minutes of the film," recalls associate producer and longtime Bruckheimer Films postproduction department head Pat Sandston, "and when they returned they decided that the film needed another huge, impressive moment that would take the form of a massive wave of dirt and debris in the wake of an asteroid hit. We considered all the great cities of the world in deciding the locale for this moment, and settled on Paris because it's so recognizable and has low buildings, which allow you to see the impact more clearly than a city with taller structures. We did a test for the actual explosion and it was so big that you couldn't see the sun for ten minutes. It worked better on the second attempt. Meanwhile, we had guys in Paris to shoot visual effects plates. And we had to put it all together in two weeks."

Postproduction for *Armageddon*, like so many other Bruckheimer productions, was a sometimes grueling process that went right down to the wire in an attempt to release the best possible film. "Jerry was at the lab with Michael Bay and myself until two o'clock in the morning," Sandston recalls, "nine days before release. Jerry doesn't do things over the telephone or from his house or office. He's in the trenches with you, and he has never tired of the process. It's a demanding, detail-oriented thing, but for every film, every TV show, every commercial, every trailer, Jerry's in there getting his point of view across, supporting his directors, and fighting for the best marketing. The process is often about conflict, but Jerry is more interested in what's the best idea. He's tenacious, his memory is unbelievable, and he doesn't let anything slide."

Armageddon's overwhelming success was bolstered even further by its wildly popular sound track. Aerosmith front man Steven Tyler recollected to *Billboard* magazine in December 2011 that key to the number-one success of the band's song "I Don't Want to Miss a Thing"—written by Diane Warren—was "the magic of [producer] Jerry Bruckheimer calling me up and saying, 'We're doing a movie called *Armageddon*. Your daughter [Liv Tyler] is in it. And I want four Aerosmith songs, plus the one you did with Diane Warren.'" The song, which would be the band's only number-one song, remained in that position on the charts for four solid weeks beginning on September 5, 1998.

ENEMY OF THE STATE: "PLANET PARANOIA"

Lightning struck twice for Bruckheimer in 1998 with his second Touchstone Pictures release, *Enemy of the State*, which reunited him with Gene Hackman, Will Smith, and, for the fifth time, director Tony Scott. Rooted firmly in the tradition of such political thrillers as *The Parallax View*, *Three Days of the Condor*, *All the President's Men*, and Oliver Stone's *JFK*—all of which trafficked in believable paranoia—the film relates the story of a rising young attorney, Robert Clayton Dean (Smith), who's framed for murder by a corrupt NSA (National Security Agency) official, Thomas Brian Reynolds (Jon Voight). To clear his name and regain his life, Dean has to turn for help to an enigmatic ex-intelligence operative known as Brill (Hackman).

Enemy of the State further advanced the big-screen career of Will Smith, while again giving Gene Hackman one of the best roles of his career. It was also the first of many films that Jon Voight would make for Bruckheimer, helping the actor enter a new and successful phase of his own long career. The film was the culmination of a long development process, which began in 1991. "It took a long time to get a screenplay," Bruckheimer explained in the film's press notes. "We started with a simple one-line idea about a man whose electronic identity is stolen and manipulated, and asked a young writer, David Marconi, to come in and develop it with us. It grew from there to encompass the more far-reaching scope of institutionalized information gathering." Once again, Bruckheimer called upon the talents of Aaron Sorkin to do another uncredited rewrite, further strengthening the material.

Certainly, the questions posed by *Enemy of the State* became even more relevant three years after it was released, when the events of September 11, 2001, gave rise to even greater issues of privacy versus protection. *Enemy of the State* also challenged the myth that Bruckheimer's films are always a target for critics. The majority of reviewers were enthusiastic about the film's canny combination of its lift-the-lid look at the internal machinations of the government's security machine, Hitchcockian suspense, Oliver Stone-esque paranoia, and pure Bruckheimer/Scott high-adrenaline action. The film won plaudits from the major critics on both coasts of the country.

Elvis Mitchell wrote in *The New York Times*: ". . . it has hurtling pace, nonstop intensity, and a stylish, appealing performance by Will Smith in his first real starring role."

And in *The Washington Post*—the major newspaper of the city in which much of the film was set—Michael O'Sullivan wrote that *Enemy of the State* was, "An enormously entertaining visit to planet paranoia."

"Planet paranoia"—also known as Earth—rewarded the film with a gross of more than $250 million worldwide.

TURN OF THE CENTURY: THREE FILMS, THREE HITS

Bruckheimer entered the new millennium with no fewer than three feature film releases, each of them vastly different in tone, subject, and genre. First up was a demolition derby lark of an action-adventure thriller for Touchstone, *Gone in Sitxy Seconds* (2000), Bruckheimer's third venture with Nicolas Cage. "After *Enemy of the State*, we were looking to lighten up a little and have some fun," says the producer. "You had to make the audience believe that they were actually going a hundred miles per hour and living the movie. We

wanted to make them feel like they were there, a ride that was on-screen rather than in an amusement park. But the movie is not just for people who love cars. It's an exciting drama about a man who wants desperately to do the right and honorable thing in life but gets drawn back into a former existence, one of crime and fear. It's a movie about making choices set against a backdrop of incredible cars."

The film was a loose remake of a 1974 action film produced, directed, written, and starring the late H. B. "Toby" Halicki that cost less than a million dollars to make and wound up grossing more than $40 million. Much beloved by automobile, racing, and demolition fans, the original *Gone in 60 Seconds* took on cult status soon after its release, but its low-rent acting by a nonprofessional cast and less-than-polished look didn't exactly endear the movie to critics.

Bruckheimer's *Gone in Sixty Seconds* was obviously a sleeker affair, but attempted to retain the raw energy of the original, or "more explosions and fewer bell-bottoms," as Jonathan Rosenbaum in the *Chicago Reader* put it. Both films feature master car thieves and lots of crashes, but the plot of the Bruckheimer version was recalibrated. Cage portrays Randall "Memphis" Raines, a retired car thief who is compelled to return to his old trade to save the life of his younger brother, Kip (Giovanni Ribisi), who is being threatened by British crime lord Raymond Vincent Calitri (Christopher Eccleston). To rescue his brother, Raines returns to Los Angeles, and, with his reunited old crew, including his mentor, Otto (Robert Duvall), and former girlfriend, Sway (Angelina Jolie), must steal fifty cars—which he decides to accomplish in one night.

Once more, Bruckheimer selected a director more rooted in short-form filmmaking than features: Dominic Sena, an award-winning, music-video helmsman, who had won some attention for his dark independent film *Kalifornia*, featuring a

pre-superstar Brad Pitt. *Gone in Sixty Seconds* didn't pretend to be anything but straight-ahead, hard-driving entertainment, with an affectionate nod to its B movie roots, while ramping it up with A movie production values. The film turned out to be another hit, garnering $101 million in domestic box office and $135 million internationally. What's more, the film arguably kicked off the first spate of street-race movies since the hot rod spectacles of the late 1950s, paving the way for the likes of The Fast and the Furious series and other urban tire-screechers.

Also released in 2000 by Touchstone was *Coyote Ugly*, which fondly and intentionally recalled *Flashdance* in that *Coyote* was another tale of a blue-collar woman who, in the course of realizing her goals, has to make a few detours in her lifestyle. But Bruckheimer also saw it in another one of his traditions: "This is a story about dreams. It's about going after your dream, and the obstacles you come up against when you're getting close to it. With a lot of effort, a little homework, and [by] keeping your eye on the prize, you can achieve whatever it is you set out to do."

The title refers to the now-legendary rough-and-tumble saloon located in the East Village area of New York City's Lower Manhattan. The film was based on an article entitled "The Muse of the Coyote Saloon," written by Elizabeth Gilbert and published in March 1997 in *GQ*, chronicling her own experiences working in the infamous establishment. Nine years later, Gilbert's book about her further life experiences, *Eat, Pray, Love*, would become a tremendous best seller, and was also made into a film.

Again, Bruckheimer turned to the advertising world, selecting as director the British-born David McNally, who had impressed audiences with a Budweiser commercial named Top Super Bowl Spot of 1999 by *Entertainment Weekly* magazine. Like other directors from Bruckheimer's previous projects, McNally would be making his first foray into film directing.

Paying homage to other films about working-class heroes, *Coyote Ugly* is a tale about Violet Sanford (Piper Perabo), a young woman who leaves her hometown and loving father (John Goodman) for the big city to make it as a songwriter. Struggling, she gets herself hired as a bartender/singer/dancer at Coyote Ugly by the owner, Lil (Maria Bello), and slowly overcomes her stage fright by strutting her stuff for the bar's boisterous patrons. The story further chronicles Violet's romance with music-industry scout Kevin O'Donnell (Adam Garcia) and concludes with her ultimate success—another Horatio Alger tale updated for a rowdy new millennium.

Coyote Ugly was a modest venture by Bruckheimer Films standards, but it still managed to bring in $113 million worldwide. Kenneth Turan of the *Los Angeles Times*, noted that the film was a ". . . very watchable piece of youthful romantic fantasy. Peppily written, *Coyote Ugly* is directed by first-timer David McNally, who brings the brisk pacing and perpetually sunny outlook of television commercials to the material at hand."

Mick LaSalle of the *San Francisco Chronicle* was refreshingly observant of why audiences have always reacted so enthusiastically to Bruckheimer's earlier films in his review:

"*Coyote Ugly* . . . has all the hallmarks of Bruckheimer, who must be considered a kind of producer-auteur at this point. . . . The temptation, the next day, is almost to deny having fun, but that would be pointless. Bruckheimer takes a simple but emotionally compelling situation and then rips through the story. It's amazing how far a movie can go on nothing but speed and directness. Other filmmakers . . . can learn a lot from watching this guy's movies."

The third film from Bruckheimer in 2000 (and the first under the family-oriented Walt Disney Pictures label) was *Remember the Titans*. It would be the producer's second cinematic examination of racial inequities in the United States, following *Dangerous Minds*. Modeled after the time-honored traditions of the all-American football movie—suspenseful games, rousing speeches, and swelling music (Trevor Rabin's "Titans Spirit" suite has been used by NBC for the closing credits of five Olympic Games broadcasts)—*Remember the Titans* nonetheless takes a clear-eyed look at the divisions and racial tensions that raged among the white and black members of a freshly desegregated team at T. C. Williams High School in Alexandria, Virginia, in 1971.

The film was based on a true story, with a screenplay by Gregory Allen Howard, an African American scripter and native Virginian who had already been turned down by almost every studio in town. But Howard's screenplay spoke directly to Bruckheimer. "All it takes is one person to like something, and you're off to the races. I read it over a weekend, and it just moved me," recalls Bruckheimer. "It was about something. It was a real event. It's a story that both kids and adults should see. It's a message of people communicating to one another and coming out winners. It's a message of triumph, and that's the kind of movie I like to see. This is not cliché; it's reality. And we're better off looking at the truth of where we are and learning to move forward. The Titans proved it's possible, and the effects of their experience are still visible in Alexandria thirty years later."

Bruckheimer elected to work with director Boaz Yakin, whose previous films had been the gritty urban dramas *Fresh* (African American backdrop) and *A Price Above Rubies* (Orthodox Jewish backdrop). Denzel Washington was cast as the new coach, Herman Boone, a relentless taskmaster determined to burst through the racial barriers to forge a strong bond between the white and black teammates. The fine supporting ensemble was, as is often seen in Bruckheimer's films, a strong sampling of veterans (Will Patton, Nicole Ari Parker) and newcomers (Ryan Gosling, Hayden Panettiere, Kip Pardue, Kate Bosworth).

Remember the Titans worked as a metaphor for the changes sweeping the American South in the early 1970s, when the aftermath of the Civil Rights struggle was already beginning to bear its initial, if painful, fruit. The film was yet another success at the box office—particularly on the basis of its very modest budget—grossing more than $115 million domestically.

"Everybody working on the picture was thrilled to be there because they knew they were going to be proud of the movie, whether it was a commercial success or not," Bruckheimer later reflected. "The fact that it's achieved the success that it has, being the underdog that it was, a movie that nobody wanted to make, thrills me. The box office is always a shock no matter what happens. If they fail, it's a shock, and if they're big hits, it's a shock. And this one, fortunately for everybody, turned out to be a picture that captured the hearts, souls, and minds of America."

AMERICANS AT WAR: THE TRIUMPH OF *BLACK HAWK DOWN* AND *PEARL HARBOR*

Remember the Titans seems a true reflection of Jerry Bruckheimer's faith in America and its diverse citizens, his fundamental belief that they can overcome barriers of prejudice and ignorance to find the greater good. Bruckheimer's America is not a place for the narrow-minded, the mean-spirited, or the intolerant. It's a land of rich rewards and victory for those who open their hearts, and then their minds, to the voices and spirits of their fellow Americans, and those around the world. These ideas would inform Jerry Bruckheimer's next two films, which were in many ways two of his most ambitious productions. Michael Bay's *Pearl Harbor* and Ridley Scott's *Black Hawk Down* (both released in 2001) were set during times of military conflict, and are a fascinating study in cinematic contrasts.

Knowing Bruckheimer's great admiration for David

Lean's historical epics, *Pearl Harbor* might be considered the producer's *Doctor Zhivago*, an emotional romantic triangle set against the backdrop of one of the most turbulent, world-changing events of the twentieth century. The essential thrust of the story was to show how a great but slumbering country suffered a shocking surprise attack from a hostile overseas force; and then, after being shaken awake, came together as a nation, girded its collective loins, and struck back with equal ferocity. The cruel irony is that *Pearl Harbor* was released in May 2001, less than four months before history seemingly repeated itself on September 11.

"*Pearl Harbor* is a seminal event in our history," notes Bruckheimer. "One of America's biggest tragedies that led to one of its greatest triumphs. This is the biggest movie I've ever attempted to make and the hardest movie I've ever had to mount for a number of reasons. But when you look at the movie, the vision is enormous. It's bigger than anything I've ever seen on-screen. I just believe in the idea, I believe in the script, I believe in the director. It's an historic movie about something that should be memorialized. We interviewed about seventy survivors of the attack, and they said, 'Make the film quick, because we're dropping like flies.'" The film, a Disney Touchstone picture, turned into quite a globe-trotting production, with filming taking place in Hawaii, California, Texas, Mexico, and Great Britain.

Despite its reliance on state-of-the-art technology and visual effects, much of *Pearl Harbor* was filmed by Michael Bay in a style that, in essence, imitates the romanticism and nobility of period U.S. military recruitment posters. The classic romantic triangle in the screenplay by Randall Wallace (*Braveheart*) involves longtime best friends and fellow pilots Rafe McCawley (Ben Affleck) and Danny Walker (Josh Hartnett), both of whom fall in love with U.S. Army nurse Evelyn Johnson (Kate Beckinsale). Their story line serves as a

soft counterpoint to the brutality of the attack itself. Through the two male protagonists, who we first see as childhood friends in a deliberately idealized American heartland, *Pearl Harbor* recounts America's journey from pre-attack innocence through a forced and very rapid wartime maturation.

With the attack, the entire timbre of the film changes. Gauzy images of biplanes lyrically flying over farm fields give way to bullets and bombs tearing into ships, buildings, and people. The tour de force depiction of the Japanese attack called upon every tool in the technological toolbox available at the time of production. And yet, the film stopped short of the graphic violence of *Saving Private Ryan* and *The Thin Red Line* in order to retain the studio-mandated PG-13 rating. Bay instead utilized sheer intensity to relay the physical damage that resulted from the attack (including a nightmarish hospital sequence shot with distorted lenses).

A crucial element of the film was the believability of the Japanese attack and the Doolittle raid on Tokyo in reprisal a few months later. Industrial Light & Magic visual effects supervisor Eric Brevig and special effects supervisor John Frazier had to imitate reality, rather than a fantasy world, with authentic-looking ships, airplanes, and landscapes. This was richly accomplished with a combination of computer-generated imagery; massive, full-size re-creations constructed on gimbals; and sophisticated, remote-controlled scale models. By any standards, the Pearl Harbor–attack sequence was a maelstrom of orchestrated mayhem. But the film also brought a sense of clarity to the chaos, allowing the viewer to follow the course of the event while retaining focus on the protagonists as they experience the horror.

When it came to casting, Bay and Bruckheimer chose strong actors who were not yet major box office draws, selecting Affleck, Hartnett, and Beckinsale to play the leads. The supporting cast was comprised of other new

faces, along with such veterans as Jon Voight (doing an uncanny impression of Franklin D. Roosevelt), Alec Baldwin (as Lieutenant Colonel James Doolittle), Dan Aykroyd, Tom Sizemore, and William Fichtner.

It's also worth noting that although *Pearl Harbor* is unabashedly and unapologetically patriotic, it neither lets America off the hook for being asleep at the wheel, nor vilifies the Japanese. Admiral Isoroku Yamamoto, the genius who reluctantly strategized and launched the attack, is portrayed by Japanese-born actor Mako as a man of honor forced by circumstance to fight a nation for which he harbors deep respect. The Japanese pilots are depicted to be as loyal and believing in their cause as their American counterparts, with the will, determination, and skill to pull off an impossible preemptive strike against their enemy.

Pearl Harbor had enthusiastic boosters among critics in the U.S. Wrote Kevin Thomas in the *Los Angeles Times*, "*Pearl Harbor* has a superb reenactment of Japan's December 7, 1941, bombing of a sizable portion of the U.S. Pacific Fleet in Honolulu, an engaging love story, and a remarkable evocation of a time when Americans virtually overnight pulled together to begin the grueling process of turning a military catastrophe into eventual triumph. The film's immense cast and crew . . . blend artistry and technology to create a blockbuster entertainment that has passion, valor, and tremendous action. Its combination of authentic aircraft and ships, stunt work, and special effects re-creates the bombing in all its precise ferocity and immense scale. And despite its scale, *Pearl Harbor* has a brisk pace that makes this three-hour war epic seem like half that time."

Once again, the success of a Jerry Bruckheimer film was measured by its popularity with audiences, and moviegoers around the world welcomed the film with nearly half a billion dollars in box office receipts. For such a homegrown

American historical drama, it may seem ironic that the foreign gross of $250 million outmatched the domestic $198 million, but Bruckheimer and Bay were, in the end, telling a story that could readily be understood by all people (including moviegoers in Japan, where *Pearl Harbor* was warmly embraced to the tune of $56.3 million, making Japan the film's number-one international market).

Bruckheimer continued on the war front with *Black Hawk Down*, but the story and film were a startling contrast to the more black-and-white conflict depicted in *Pearl Harbor*. Set in 1993, at a time when America was experiencing the morally and politically convoluted military conflicts that followed the clear-cut virtues of fighting the Second World War, this remarkably accomplished account of the Battle of Mogadishu (Somalia) now stands as one of Bruckheimer's greatest accomplishments. It's also one of the first depictions of modern post-Vietnam combat, warfare in an age where high-tech surveillance and video games almost blur . . . until the real bullets begin to hit human flesh.

Ironically, *Black Hawk Down* may not have found its way to the screen save for Jerry Bruckheimer's legendary tenacity and diplomacy. After Disney declined to produce the project, Bruckheimer was faced with quite the challenge. "I remember that we were deep into preproduction on the film when we received word that Disney was not going to proceed with the movie," recalls KristieAnne Reed, then working in JBF's feature division and now executive vice president of Jerry Bruckheimer Television. "This was just before we were headed to Kentucky on our annual company retreat, so the timing was really uncomfortable. When we got to the farm, I remember Jerry on one phone line, Mike Stenson on another, and Chad Oman on the third, all trying to keep the film alive. I remember thinking, 'Dear lord, what will we do?'

"But by the time the dinner bell rang," Reed continues, "everything was completely settled. The film was set up at Columbia Pictures and Revolution Studios, and Jerry never broke a sweat. He always has this calm attitude of 'we'll get it done, we'll figure it out,' and this story kind of typifies that. He is the ultimate problem solver and strategist, and if you tell him the sky is falling, he'll look at you and say, 'Don't worry, you'll figure it out.'"

Although Bruckheimer ultimately collaborated with Tony Scott on six films, *Black Hawk Down* is, to date, his only partnership with Scott's older brother, Ridley (now Sir Ridley) Scott, and the merging of their sensibilities would result in a film that was successful both in tone and artistry. *Black Hawk Down* was at once a deeply moving tribute to the American soldiers who, having arrived in Somalia on a humanitarian mission, were then forced to battle their way out of Mogadishu, one of the most hostile cities on earth; it was also an objective study of men at war in a far-off place that is culturally, ethnically, and politically almost totally alien.

Based on a nonfiction book by Mark Bowden, *Black Hawk Down* is the account of a group of elite U.S. soldiers sent into Mogadishu, Somalia, in October 1993 as part of a United Nations peacekeeping operation. Their mission was to abduct two top lieutenants of the Somali warlord Muhammad Farrah Aidid as part of a strategy to quell the civil war and help those suffering through a famine that is ravaging the country. The U.S. troops had come to Somalia with good intentions, hoping to save lives—and not take them. But increasingly mired in the incomprehensible, feudal politics of Somalia—in which one clan has been pitted against another for a millennium—the soldiers are instead destined to get a brutal education when the carefully planned mission takes unexpected turns, resulting in the U.S. military's single biggest firefight since Vietnam.

Black Hawk Down methodically follows numerous American soldiers, step-by-step, throughout the Battle of Mogadishu, on the ground and in the air. Much of the story is experienced through the eyes of Staff Sergeant Matt Eversmann (Josh Hartnett), an idealistic young ranger whose mettle is sorely tested when he is unexpectedly handed command of one of the four "Chalks" assigned to secure the target building. However, we also experience the event with a myriad of other characters, including a few Somalis who succinctly express enough of their point of view to allow the audience to see the event from the "other side."

From the time he read Bowden's book in galley form, Bruckheimer knew that it was a project he wanted to get on-screen. "I read the book before it came out in bookstores and fell in love with it," says the producer. "I've always liked to tell stories that involve brotherhood amongst men, caring about somebody else's life more than you care about your own. And that's what these Rangers, Delta Force soldiers, and pilots did. It was more important to get their buddy home alive than it was to save themselves. It's heroism under fire, and that's a powerful subject for any film."

One problem faced by Scott, Bruckheimer, and their screenwriters, Ken Nolan and Steve Zaillian, was boiling down the battle and the huge number of personalities that populated Bowden's book into a dramatically viable format. "Condensing these events into two or two-and-a-half hours was difficult," Bruckheimer comments. "We knew that a certain amount of creative license would have to be taken, telescoping events and compositing some of the real people involved in the battle. You have to make choices while staying true to the subject, and hopefully we've made the right ones. The book follows the fortunes of almost a hundred soldiers, and, of course, that would have been impossible on film. I think that what's remarkable about the screenplay is that we still get to know forty characters, and live the battle through their experiences."

The mammoth cast of speaking players was recruited

from many countries in addition to the U.S., so several actors had to learn to quash their native accents (British, Australian, Danish, etc.) in favor of an American vernacular. Josh Hartnett, fresh from starring in *Pearl Harbor*, was selected to portray Sergeant Eversmann. He was joined by a veritable who's who of acting talent, including Eric Bana, Ewan McGregor, Jeremy Piven, Sam Shepard, Jason Isaacs, Tom Hardy, Nikolaj Coster-Waldau, and *Pearl Harbor* veterans Tom Sizemore, William Fichtner, and Ewen Bremner, plus young actors who would later appear in future Bruckheimer productions, including Orlando Bloom, Hugh Dancy, and Gabriel Casseus. In this bewildering collection of soldiers, the two most representative figures are Eversmann—idealistic, respectful of the Somalis, and sensitive to their plight, but inexperienced in combat—and "Hoot" Gibson (Bana), a Delta Force operator and ultimate soldier who knows that "once that first bullet goes past your head, politics and all that shit just go right out the window." This is a sentiment reiterated in the film's denouement when Hoot tells Eversmann, when explaining why he continues fighting, "It's about the men next to you. That's all it is."

Black Hawk Down does take a stand squarely on the side of the Americans, who are in Somalia to alleviate the genocidal starvation of thousands while warlords fight among themselves. But it's also a film about soldiers of every uniform, who are each devoted to their own countries and causes. The extraordinarily graphic violence in *Black Hawk Down* certainly marks it as a kind of antiwar film—in no way can a film that depicts such horrors be accused of being "pro war"— but Ridley Scott never indulges in sentimental platitudes about the evils of battle. As a student of history, he knows that war is as endemic to the human condition as eating and procreating. (The film actually opens with Plato's quote, "Only the dead have seen the end of war.") *Black Hawk Down* honors the

American soldiers who place such high value on human life with their "No man left behind" credo but also explores the terrible irony that they are forced to take life away from others.

The filming of *Black Hawk Down* occurred under remarkably difficult circumstances in Morocco, primarily in the teeming seaside working-class enclave of Sidi Moussa, a rough neighborhood in the suburb of Salé, across the Bou Regreg River from the capital of Rabat. There, production designer Arthur Max re-created Mogadishu with both new constructions (particularly the impressive target building), and a creative overlay of existing apartment buildings and shops with Somali signage and other design flourishes. In circumstances that are now unbelievable in the post-9/11 world, an actual U.S. military deployment was enacted in Rabat for the "insertion" scene in which the Rangers and Delta Force soldiers fast-rope from Black Hawk helicopters to the target building.

Of all the Herculean tasks facing Jerry Bruckheimer and Ridley Scott, none were so great as the extraordinary negotiations among the production staff, the Moroccan government, the U.S. State Department, and the U.S. Department of Defense. These sensitive talks were had in the hope of allowing approximately one hundred U.S. Rangers, four Black Hawks, and four MH-6 "Little Bird" helicopters and their pilots from the 160th Special Operations Aviation Regiment (SOAR)—plus all of the backup military personnel accompanying them—to fly across the Atlantic and help the production properly re-create the first several minutes and other key moments of the mission with utmost verisimilitude.

This was no small matter. Even before recent events, the notion of bringing armed forces and matériel from the United States to a sovereign North African kingdom with a Muslim population—however friendly relations might be between the countries—was far-reaching, to say the least.

"However enthusiastic the government was about our project," Jerry Bruckheimer recalls, "there were still bureaucracies to deal with, and there were many voices to be heard on the matter. There were a lot of issues that had to be worked out between the State Department and the Moroccan government, and it took a lot longer than we'd expected.

"There were so many issues, such as security," Bruckheimer continues. "Who would protect the helicopters and the men? Where were they going to be quartered? How many days of filming would they be required to participate in? All of these details had to be minutely worked out in advance, and even though we have a great relationship with the government, this was a much bigger operation than anything we had attempted before, even on *Top Gun* and *Pearl Harbor*. We were talking about actual troop deployment."

A combination of Bruckheimer's close relationship with the U.S. military, forged on films like *Top Gun* and *Pearl Harbor*, and Scott's friendship with Moroccan authorities at the highest levels, resulted in something truly unprecedented. Finally, word came through that all necessary paperwork had received the signatures of top U.S. and Moroccan authorities (including King Mohammed VI), and two C-5 transport planes landed at an airport near Rabat, delivering their cargo: more than one hundred soldiers from the Third Battalion, Bravo Company of the Seventy-Fifth Ranger regiment—the same company that actually fought in Mogadishu—four Black Hawks and four Little Birds, ready for duty, along with their pilots from the 160th SOAR. Each Black Hawk had its own name emblazoned just below the rotor blades: Nightstalker, Black Scorpion, and—by some incredible coincidence—Armageddon and Gladiator, the titles of, respectively, a Jerry Bruckheimer film and a Ridley Scott film.

With the advent of 9/11 just two months after the film wrapped, and the subsequent war on terrorism that has now lasted for over a decade, such a deployment is today virtually inconceivable. And sadly, nearly twenty years after the events depicted in the film, Somalia is still a country in the throes of violence and anarchy, and now best known for its modern-day pirates raiding ships in the waters off its coastline.

Black Hawk Down was released at the end of December 2001 in only four theaters, in order for it to qualify for immediate Academy Award consideration, and the film received four nods, including Best Director and Best Cinematography (Slawomir Idziak). It won for both Best Editing (Pietro Scalia) and Best Sound. After it went into general release in mid-January 2002, the film grossed $172 million worldwide, a mighty sum for such a demanding story.

With *Black Hawk Down*, Jerry Bruckheimer finally enjoyed the critical recognition that comes with the making of an acknowledged cinematic masterpiece. In the *Los Angeles Times*, Kenneth Turan spoke for many when he wrote that, ". . . as much as a movie ever has, it puts you completely inside that event, brilliantly taking you where most people, even those who were actually there, wouldn't want to be. For 'realism' is a mild word for the way director Ridley Scott sweepingly re-creates 1993's fierce fifteen-hour battle . . . his is a triumph of pure filmmaker, a pitiless, unrelenting, no-excuses war movie so thoroughly convincing it's frequently difficult to believe it is a staged re-creation. *Black Hawk Down* can be tough to sit through, but the fluidity and skill involved are so impressive it's an exhilarating experience as well."

Turan also wrote, "Though the result is much closer to *Battle of Algiers* than *Pearl Harbor*, the film is also an unlikely triumph for producer Jerry Bruckheimer . . . the producer understood what was called for here, and he put his extensive experience to use in getting the project what it needed, including cajoling the Army into providing Rangers and Black Hawk helicopters and persuading the king of Morocco,

where the film was shot, to allow these troops onto his soil."

CHANGING THE PACE

After the extraordinarily demanding, even exhausting, shoots of *Pearl Harbor* and *Black Hawk Down*, Bruckheimer decided to follow with two films that were more modest and lighthearted. The action-comedy *Bad Company* (2002) returned the producer to Disney's Touchstone Pictures and matched stars Anthony Hopkins and Chris Rock with director Joel Schumacher (*The Lost Boys*, *A Time to Kill*, *Batman Forever*). The filmmakers deliberately paired one of the screen's most heralded veteran actors, Hopkins, with a brash newcomer, Rock, whose profane stand-up broadsides reminded many of Eddie Murphy's brand of humor.

In the story, Rock portrays Jake Hayes, the irresponsible twin brother of a murdered CIA agent. He is enlisted to replace his late brother by a CIA agent named Oakes (Hopkins). The action takes Hayes and Oakes to Prague, Czech Republic, and then to New York, where they have to foil a terrorist bomb plot. And therein lies one of the reasons for the film's lack of success; it was originally scheduled to be released in December 2001, but the events of 9/11 hardly put audiences in the mood to watch a piece of entertainment, amusing or serious, about terrorist activity in New York, and that mood hadn't changed when the film opened in June 2002.

Bruckheimer was obviously disappointed, but took it in stride. "It was the wrong time and the wrong place for *Bad Company*, which was merely designed to be a fun piece of entertainment. I think you look back and try to learn from your mistakes. In the end, maybe *Bad Company* didn't have enough comedy to be a comedy, and not enough action to be an action movie. It was a fun and entertaining movie, but just didn't really catch on with the audience."

Similarly lighthearted—but more successful—was the

screwball comedy *Kangaroo Jack* (2003), a fish-out-of-water story about two B-grade crooks from Brooklyn, best buddies Charlie Carbone and Louis Booker (Jerry O'Connell and Anthony Anderson, respectively). They are sent Down Under by Charlie's stepfather, crime boss Sal Maggio (Christopher Walken), to make a personal cash delivery to an enigmatic "Mr. Smith."

On the road in the outback, Charlie and Louis accidentally hit a kangaroo. Louis puts his lucky red jacket (emblazoned with BROOKLYN on the front) on the "dead" creature for a little photo session. But the kangaroo soon recovers and then hops away with the thick wad of cash that Louis had left in the jacket's pocket. Now it's Charlie and Louis's turn to chase down "Kangaroo Jack" and recover the cash before "Mr. Smith" chases them down.

"Charlie and Louis are the quintessential strangers in a strange land," says Bruckheimer, "and when you add the unpredictability of an untamed animal to the mix, the stakes are raised even higher. The more over-the-top their predicament, the funnier it gets."

Directed by *Coyote Ugly*'s David McNally and released by Warner Bros., *Kangaroo Jack* is a classic case of how a bird can change its feathers. Filmed under the title *Down and Under*, Bruckheimer and his team discovered in early test screenings that audiences especially responded to the film's kangaroo. There ensued considerable reworking to increase the role of the creature, resulting in the rambunctious marsupial taking a much more prominent position in the tale. Warner Bros. also suggested using the word "kangaroo" in the title to capitalize on the animal's appeal for the marketing of the film. A live kangaroo portrayed "Jackie Legs" in some scenes, but other footage required the use of a robotic figure.

"I was the executive on the movie in Australia," recalls KristieAnne Reed, "and we had originally intended to use both a live and an animatronic kangaroo. So of course, we get there, and the first scene they shoot with the mechanical kangaroo 'stuffy' doesn't work at all. I call Jerry and say, 'The kangaroo looks like a robot, what do I do?' And he said, 'Shoot the scene with the stuffy, then pull the kangaroo out and shoot it again on an empty visual effects plate.' Hoyt Yeatman had already pioneered computer graphics creature technology with *Mighty Joe Young*, and he was confident that he could convincingly create a kangaroo that could have its own life and character, and Jerry was willing to put his faith in Hoyt's abilities."

Bruckheimer's adventurous approach paid off handsomely. The modestly budgeted *Kangaroo Jack* opened at number one in mid-January 2003 and was popular enough for Warner Bros. (for whom Bruckheimer made the film on another temporary leave from Disney) to make an animated sequel the following year, although not with the producer's participation.

Bruckheimer's next 2003 release was also off the beaten path for him, but yet another sign of his desire to explore beyond the parameters long associated with his brand. Made on a relatively low budget and intimately scaled, *Veronica Guerin* was based on the true story of the fiery and fearless Irish journalist whose investigations into the Dublin underworld and drug trade for the *Sunday Independent* newspaper ended with her murder in 1996. Joel Schumacher directed once again for Bruckheimer, and the filmmakers cast an actress of uncommon power and presence, Cate Blanchett, in the title role. She was backed by a superb company of Irish performers, among them Gerard McSorley, as drug lord and Guerin nemesis John Gilligan, Ciarán Hinds, Brenda Fricker, and, in an unbilled cameo, Colin Farrell (whose U.S. career was launched by Schumacher in *Tigerland* and *Phone Booth*).

Ironically, a man long associated with producing testosterone-packed male fantasies had now produced a motion picture about one of the strongest-willed, real-life heroines in recent history. "I like to make movies about people who make a difference," he notes. "The reason I was attracted to *Veronica Guerin* is that it's a story of courage and bravery about a woman who just couldn't live with the truth without exposing it. And that to me is something I had to see on-screen, because I love individuals like that. I thought that her story was incredibly powerful and deserved to be told to a wider audience outside of Ireland."

Veronica Guerin took more than a few chances, not the least of which was the depiction of its title character as someone much less than saintly. And yet she was putting her very life on the line to combat an evil that was burning its way into the heart of Irish society, and destroying the life of Dublin's working-class youth.

" . . . The finest honor director Joel Schumacher and screenwriters Carol Doyle and Mary Agnes Donoghue pay her," noted Lisa Schwarzbaum in her review of *Veronica Guerin* for *Entertainment Weekly*, "and an audience who may be learning about her work for the first time is this: There's no airbrushing of character. She's played with intelligence whipped clean of any airs and poses by the always cleanly intelligent Cate Blanchett, who makes Guerin a 3-D woman, not a 2-D heroine." The critic also noted of the Touchstone Pictures film, ". . . the film evades sensationalism even when the subject's chutzpah is sensational."

"One of the most emotional screenings I've ever been to in my life was when we had the Irish premiere," recalls Bruckheimer. "You could just feel a hush come over everyone when the lights went out. You could feel the tension in the crowd. At the end of it, there was thunderous applause. We brought Veronica's family up onstage, and then Cate Blanchett, who got a ten-minute standing ovation. That gives you a sense of how much the Irish people appreciated the movie and her performance. Bernie Guerin, Veronica's mother, told me that

one out of four people in Ireland saw the picture, which is quite a statistic. And not everything can be judged in dollars and cents. I'm very proud of the film and what it accomplished."

PIRATES OF THE CARIBBEAN AND KING ARTHUR: RETURN TO EPICS

Very much contrasting with *Veronica Guerin* in every conceivable way was the third of Bruckheimer's 2003 releases, *Pirates of the Caribbean: The Curse of the Black Pearl*, the first of a franchise that would inexorably alter the landscape of his career, and movies in general. The fourth JBF film of that momentous year was the second entry in yet another franchise, *Bad Boys II*, which gave the producer two massive consecutive hits. (Both films are explored in detail in the Franchise chapter.)

King Arthur (2004) was yet another study in contrasts to nearly every previous attempt to put the Matter of Britain on-screen (more than a hundred since the first recorded effort, *Launcelot and Elaine*, in 1909). The screenplay by David Franzoni, who won an Academy Award for Ridley Scott's *Gladiator* four years earlier, resulted in a film that, per Todd McCarthy's review in *Variety*, " . . . bracingly repositions the Arthurian myth in a specific and savage historical moment quite removed from its usual placement in a bucolic world of chivalrous knights, a mischievous magician, and an errant queen. Impressively made and well acted by an exceedingly attractive cast, this dark tale of ceaseless conflict is adult entertainment."

"With *King Arthur*, we tried to tell the definitive story of the leader and warrior who emerged to lead the Britons against the Saxons," says Bruckheimer. "That's what excited me about this film—it's a new look at a tale that we thought we were familiar with. The truth is that King Arthur lived in a much earlier time period than you see in most of the movie versions—the Dark Ages. David Franzoni worked out a new approach to the subject matter that offered a more historically accurate story of King Arthur."

King Arthur, from Touchstone, is steeped in fifth-century A.D. Roman and British history, with the title character, known as Lucius Artorius Castus (Clive Owen in his first mainstream starring role), the commander of a detachment of the Sarmatian knights. He and his fellow soldiers are a kind of Roman special-forces unit guarding Hadrian's Wall against the Saxons, and sometimes battling the indigenous Celtic tribes. In addition to Keira Knightley, who had just leapt to stardom in *Pirates of the Caribbean: The Curse of the Black Pearl*, the cast also included Hugh Dancy, who had appeared in *Black Hawk Down* and would later star with Isla Fisher in *Confessions of a Shopaholic*, and in a performance of offbeat, underplayed brilliance, Stellan Skarsgard, previous to his appearances as Bootstrap Bill in the second and third entries of the Pirates of the Caribbean series.

The unorthodox choice of director was Antoine Fuqua, whose tales of contemporary urban life, such as *Training Day*, marked him as someone who could bring some grit and authenticity to a less than decorous period of history.

Considering a much more receptive international market to historically themed films, it's not surprising that *King Arthur* grossed three times the amount worldwide as it did domestically, bringing in more than $200 million. The graphic violence was toned down for the film's PG-13–rated theatrical release, but the "director's cut," as issued on DVD, was fifteen minutes longer and more indicative of the film that had actually been filmed on so epic a scale in Ireland and Great Britain.

A NEW FRANCHISE IS BORN . . . AND DOWN THE *GLORY ROAD*

Yet another large-scale adventure premiered in 2004,

the first in a new Bruckheimer/Disney blockbuster franchise: *National Treasure* (see the Franchise chapter). The following year would see no actual releases, although the mammoth combined shoot of *Pirates of the Caribbean: Dead Man's Chest* and *Pirates of the Caribbean: At World's End* commenced in the West Indies, the Bahamas, and Los Angeles, as did filming for two releases scheduled for 2006.

Glory Road was rooted squarely in the tradition of *Remember the Titans*, another modestly proportioned film for Walt Disney Pictures that combined sports, history, and social commentary without one theme canceling out the other. The film was set in 1966, two years after the Civil Rights Act had passed, although it had not yet been embraced by a substantial number of Americans. *Glory Road* tells the true story of Texas Western College (now the University of Texas at El Paso) basketball coach Don Haskins (Josh Lucas) and his decision to go into the championship with a team whose starting five were all African American, for the first time in NCAA history. The tough, color-blind Haskins was crucial in changing the perception of black athletes by white America, and was a major catalyst to activating the very principles that the Civil Rights Act represented.

This rousingly inspirational story, based on Haskins's own autobiographical book, really captured Bruckheimer's imagination. "What's so interesting about Don Haskins is that he wasn't looking to make any kind of statement. He simply was driven to win," says the producer. "Yet in making winning his priority, he changed history. Prior to Haskins's heartfelt decision to have an all African American starting lineup at the championship game, there were many opportunities missed by gifted athletes. Haskins's actions inspired a lot of players to go on and have illustrious NBA careers. He was an amazing person who had an indelible impact on a lot of lives."

Bruckheimer continues, "I think this is an especially

important story to tell today because a lot of kids no longer realize how hard the players and coaches in the sixties had to fight to bring them the incredible opportunities that exist now."

In developing the story of the 1966 NCAA championship and turning it into a feature film, Bruckheimer always saw it as being much broader than simply a "sports drama." He saw it as being about the human drive to excel. "Don Haskins is a fascinating character: a hard-charger and a tough personality who demanded a lot from the people around him," observes Bruckheimer. "He understood something very key—which is that to become a champion, it takes a lot of character and a lot of hard work. That is what lies at the heart of this story. Any way we can integrate society and take away the prejudice is better for all of us."

Yet another director of commercials, James Gartner, was selected by Bruckheimer to make his feature-film debut with *Glory Road*, and with him he brought a refreshing lack of clichés to what might have been an overly sentimental enterprise. With a strong supporting cast—led by Bruckheimer mainstay Jon Voight as Adolph Rupp, the legendary coach of the then all-white University of Kentucky Wildcats (the opposing team in the championships)—*Glory Road* elicited a great many fine reviews. "It's one helluva story," wrote Ann Hornaday in *The Washington Post*, "and if this moving, and even thrilling little movie finally brings Haskins and a truly great American sports story to light, then three cheers and hooray."

In the *Chicago Sun-Times*, Roger Ebert wrote, ". . . the movie is not really about underdogs and winning the big game. It's about racism in American sports . . . As the end credits tell us what happened in later life to the members of that 1966 Texas Western team, we realize that Haskins not only won an NCAA title but made a contribution to the future that is still being realized."

Glory Road proudly took its place alongside *Dangerous Minds*, *Remember the Titans*, *Pearl Harbor*, and *Black Hawk Down* as a thoughtful meditation on current or recent events that forever changed the internal fiber of America.

DÉJÀ VU: REUNION WITH DENZEL WASHINGTON AND TONY SCOTT

Déjà Vu, the producer's second release of 2006, brought together Jerry Bruckheimer and director Tony Scott for a sixth collaboration. It was also their second film with Denzel Washington since *Crimson Tide* ten years earlier. A smart action-fantasy entertainment movie that was deemed by Robert Koehler in his *Variety* review to be an "exquisitely rendered . . . existential sci-fi thriller sure to elicit post-screening discussions . . ." *Déjà Vu* (from Touchstone Pictures) was a fanciful mind-bender written by Bill Marsilii and Terry Rossio (one half of the brilliant Rossio/Elliott team that scribed the first four Pirates of the Caribbean films).

Marsilii and Rossio's concept was unique: an unconventional, intricately woven thriller/love-story that takes place unmoored from the usual rules of time. Starting with a deadly, heartbreaking tragedy, a federal agent (Washington) has to follow his sense of déjà vu and, using top secret technology, trace his steps all the way back to the moment in time when he might have a shot at altering the catastrophe—and with it, his own chance for a once-in-a-lifetime love affair.

Recalls Bruckheimer, "The concept of *Déjà Vu* was completely original, a real page-turner, and different from any other love story I had ever read. We were fortunate enough to be the first ones to get a peek at it, so we bought the screenplay within forty-eight hours of receiving it."

Déjà Vu is notable for having been the first film to shoot in New Orleans after the ravages of Hurricane Katrina, and proved to be a tremendous financial and psychological boon for the city. Filming was set to begin in the fall of 2005, but in late August, Katrina smashed into the city, reducing parts of it to a flooded ruin. Bruckheimer and Scott originally considered other locations in the aftermath, but finally agreed that there was no place in the country that compared to the look and atmosphere of New Orleans. And what's more, nothing would be better for the Crescent City than an infusion of support—financial and otherwise. Recalls Bruckheimer, "I was already in love with New Orleans, having made several films there. Tony had never been there before, but he too fell in love with all the French and Spanish influences. The city has a distinct culture that is unforgettable, and Tony and I both knew this was right for the story of *Déjà Vu*. New Orleans deservedly became a character in the film."

Keeping in close contact with the New Orleans Film Commission, Bruckheimer and Scott delayed filming until early 2006, when the infrastructure of the city was beginning to be rebuilt. For the producer and the entire company, it was a richly rewarding experience. "While filming on the streets of New Orleans, everyday local people would thank us for bringing the film there and helping to revitalize a city in need," says Bruckheimer. "Tony and I, and the cast and crew, all felt very proud to be part of the rebirth of a great city, and the return of the film industry there."

The complex script by Marsilii and Rossio—which William Arnold of the *Seattle Post-Intelligencer* called "unusually intelligent and challenging for a big-budget Hollywood thriller"—incorporates and mixes elements of police work, domestic terrorism, science fiction, and romance in a highly original brew. It presented to audiences a time-travel story miles away from the likes of *The Time Machine* or *Somewhere in Time* (although like both films, a love story was at the heart of the fantasy). Once again, Denzel Washington (as ATF Agent Doug Carlin) lit up a Bruckheimer/Tony Scott collaboration with his charisma and skill, and critics responded accordingly. William Arnold described *Déjà Vu* as "super-producer Jerry Bruckheimer's lavishly mounted, compulsively excited and intellectually intriguing year-end thriller."

Bruckheimer's predilection for "hiring the best of the best" paid off once again, as *Déjà Vu* brought in a total of $180 million worldwide.

BRANCHING OUT: COMEDY, ANIMATION, AND FANTASY

The next two Bruckheimer/Disney releases were the juggernaut sequels *Pirates of the Caribbean: Dead Man's Chest* (2006) and *Pirates of the Caribbean: At World's End* (2007), which toppled a considerable number of box office records and made a huge dent in the international consciousness. The franchise steamroller continued on in 2007 with *National Treasure: Book of Secrets*, yet another blockbuster.

But two years later, events of the day conspired to roadblock Bruckheimer's initial foray into light romantic comedy, the screen version of Sophie Kinsella's massively successful novel (and the first of an equally successful series of five, which sold millions worldwide), *Confessions of a Shopaholic* (2009). This breezy account of the professional and romantic misadventures of Rebecca Bloomwood, the obsessive fashionista of the title, was brought to the screen by director P. J. Hogan (*My Best Friend's Wedding*). The gifted Isla Fisher was cast in the title role, and the strong supporting cast included Hugh Dancy (*Black Hawk Down* and *King Arthur*), John Goodman (*Coyote Ugly*), Joan Cusack, Kristin Scott Thomas, and John Lithgow. Originally for Disney's Touchstone division, it was later transferred to Walt Disney Pictures, with the film intended for a wider audience, including fashion-minded teenage girls.

"We're always looking for fresh ideas," says Bruckheimer, "and taking on a romantic comedy was new for us, which I found really exciting. Madeleine Wickham [Sophie Kinsella is her pen name] was a big force in helping us develop the screenplay through many years of development, and working with us throughout the movie to make sure that Rebecca Bloomwood and all of the other characters in the story came to life the way she envisioned them when she wrote the novel. Obviously, a novel is much longer than a movie, so you have to condense and shorten things, and we also changed the locale from London to New York, but we made sure that Maddy was involved to ensure that we were true to the spirit of her novels."

The resulting film was charming, sweet-spirited, and truly romantic, with suitably outrageous clothing designs by the edgy Patricia Field, dazzling New York locations to die for, and a deliberate nod to the sort of fast-talking, quick-moving comedies of the past that Preston Sturges and Frank Capra may have recognized. And the only explosion in the film was the opening of Becky Bloomwood's wardrobe. But in between the start of production and its February 2009 release date, America (and much of the world with it) had plunged into what's since become widely known as "The Great Recession." And with millions out of work, homes in foreclosure, and shuttered storefronts, the country was in little mood to enjoy a comedy about the pursuit of materialism.

"The shame of it," recalls Bruckheimer, "is that the film was about the very things that got us in such a mess, all embodied by Becky. She maxes out her credit cards, spends what she doesn't have, and fools herself into thinking that consumerism and materialism are substitutes for real values. By the end of the film, she's learned several valuable lessons, but the country just wasn't in the mood to laugh with and at her."

Confessions of a Shopaholic certainly did have its admirers, among them Owen Gleiberman of *Entertainment Weekly*, who confirmed Bruckheimer's assessment in his review: "*Confessions of a Shopaholic* may have been shot before the economic crisis, but as the cautionary tale of one girl's protracted shopping meltdown, it's actually quite timely." Gleiberman also praised the prodigious comedic skills of Isla Fisher, noting that, "Breathless and petite, yet powerfully in-your-face, Fisher combines dizzy femininity and no-nonsense verve in the manner of a classic screwball heroine. She's like Carole Lombard reborn as a tiny angel-faced dynamo."

In the *Chicago Sun-Times*, Roger Ebert also noted the film's effective updating of the hallmarks of classic '30s and '40s screwball comedy: "It glories in its silliness, and the actors are permitted the sort of goofy acting that distinguished screwball comedy. We get double takes, slow burns, pratfalls, exploding clothes wardrobes, dropped trays, tear-away dresses, missing maids of honor, overnight fame, public disgrace, and not, amazingly, a single obnoxious cat or dog."

Continuing his experiments with previously unexplored genres (for him), Bruckheimer then released in 2009 an energetic Walt Disney Pictures family movie, the part live-action/part digital animated 3-D adventure comedy *G-Force*. A two-time Academy Award-winning and highly innovative visual effects supervisor, director Hoyt Yeatman had a long history with Bruckheimer that included *Crimson Tide*, *The Rock*, *Con Air*, *Armageddon*, and *Kangaroo Jack*. The idea for *G-Force* was actually conceived by Yeatman's then six-year-old son. *G-Force* is about a crack team of highly trained commandos seeking to prevent a ruthless billionaire from taking over the world. The twist is that the commando team is comprised of three guinea pigs, a mole, and a fly. Part of the fun in *G-Force* was to see a Bruckheimer film make affectionate fun of action-movie conventions that were, to a great extent, laid down by the producer himself in past films. The filmmakers even included some direct dialogue references to Bruckheimer's previous productions (i.e. "Leave no rodent behind," echoing

Black Hawk Down's quote, "Leave no man behind").

"I've always loved adventure films," says Bruckheimer, "but if you can approach the genre from a different angle than what's been seen previously, the possibilities are even more exciting. That's what we tried to do with the Pirates of the Caribbean films, combining the classic buccaneer genre with supernatural elements and lots of offbeat comedy. It's fun to take films based on familiar, even classic themes, give them a twist, and see what evolves. Movies about secret agents have been with us on-screen long before James Bond, and they seem to be as popular now as they've ever been. And movies, either animated or live-action, in which animals speak and have personalities of their own, have also been with us for quite some time.

"What we've never seen, however," he continues, "is a movie about secret agents who also happen to be animals, and what's more, in a combination of live-action, animation, and digital 3-D."

Bruckheimer and Yeatman assembled topflight voice and live-action talent for *G-Force*, including Nicolas Cage, Penélope Cruz, Sam Rockwell, Tracy Morgan, Jon Favreau, and Steve Buscemi (as the voices of the animals), and on-screen performers such as Zach Galifianakis (pre-*The Hangover*), Bill Nighy (who had been digitized as Davy Jones in the second and third Pirates of the Caribbean opuses), and Will Arnett. The effects from Sony Pictures Imageworks were state of the art, as the digital 3-D pictures conversion was done with the greatest care (and, innovatively, the first time in which the images "broke the frame," actually exceeding the conventional screen framing).

"With *G-Force*," notes Bruckheimer, "we just wanted to appeal to everyone from six to sixty. We also wanted to break down a few walls between the viewer and the screen, and to bring the audience closer to the action. Considering that we shot the film in 2-D, and did a very careful 3-D conversion, I think we succeeded on many levels. It was a fun ride."

G-Force proved to be popular with kids and their parents, resulting in a worldwide take of just under $300 million. The guinea pigs had truly spoken an international language.

In 2010, Jerry Bruckheimer Films was responsible for not one, but two huge summer tent-pole epics designed for those "six to sixty" audiences. Greatly different in subject matter, the two films nonetheless shared a common theme that could easily apply to the producer himself: discovering one's destiny and full potential, not alone, but with the help of friends and lovers.

With *Prince of Persia: The Sands of Time*, Bruckheimer once again dredged a dormant genre out of its long sleep. "I've always enjoyed adapting the kinds of films I loved watching as a youngster growing up in Detroit and giving them a swift kick to bring them up to the standards of contemporary moviemaking," says the producer. "For example, in the mid-1980s, no one was making movies about pilots testing the limits of their courage, as they were at the dawn of the jet age in the 1950s. We made *Top Gun*. By the mid-1990s, Cold War suspense movies had expired with the fall of the Soviet Union. We made *Crimson Tide*. Science fiction movies had dropped off in popularity by the late 1990s. We made *Armageddon*. In the first decade of the twenty-first century, pirate movies had long since walked the plank as a viable movie genre. We made *Pirates of the Caribbean: The Curse of the Black Pearl*, and then two more in a series, which, much to our surprise and joy, became a cultural phenomenon. Everyone said that nobody would be interested in watching a movie about history hunters who use their brains rather than brawn to uncover present-day mysteries about the past. We made *National Treasure* and *National Treasure: Book of Secrets*," Bruckheimer recounts.

"It had been a very long time since the wonderfully magical and colorful world of the ancient Near East had been deemed a suitable backdrop for a major motion picture. Perhaps this is the result of recent history and geopolitics," says the producer. "But in 1989, a very creative and imaginative young man named Jordan Mechner drew on the beauty and mythology of ancient Persia as the foundation of a brand-new kind of video game, which he titled *Prince of Persia*. This presented us with a wonderful opportunity to use the world that Jordan had created as a springboard for an exciting fantasy adventure film which—just as we paid homage to the original Disneyland attraction in the Pirates of the Caribbean films while inventing something fresh and new—would allow us to reinvent an entire genre. We tried to combine the special world that Jordan conjured up in his games with the magnificent history, legend, and lore of ancient Persia."

The film's script was developed over many years with such writers as the aforementioned Mechner, Boaz Yakin, and the team of Doug Miro and Carlo Bernard, but one constant thread was retained throughout: the Dagger of Time. This magical object was the key element of *The Sands of Time*, the first Prince of Persia video game that Mechner did for Ubisoft. The dagger gives its possessor the ability to reverse time—but only for a few moments—by pressing a jewel on the top of its handle.

In choosing a director, Bruckheimer departed from his long tradition of hiring newcomers from the world of commercials and music videos. Going quite in the opposite direction, he instead selected Mike Newell, a British veteran who had demonstrated unusual versatility throughout his career, with feature film credits going back three decades and ranging from *Four Weddings and a Funeral* to *Donnie Brasco* to *Harry Potter and the Goblet of Fire*. "Mike can do just about any kind of movie," Bruckheimer notes. "He has a really wonderful palette that he paints from, and that's very important to us. We wanted an entertaining film that appeals to a broad audience, but also

something special that concentrates on character and story."

For the leading role of Dastan, the street urchin adopted into the royal family of Persia and then falsely accused of the murder of his own father, the king, Bruckheimer once again cast against type by selecting Jake Gyllenhaal. Known up to that point primarily for his serious and demanding performances in projects such as *Donnie Darko*, *Brokeback Mountain*, *Jarhead*, and *Zodiac*, Gyllenhaal was to be converted into a full-blown action star over the course of production, his natural athleticism coming into full play with Dastan's fighting and acrobatic skills. Drawing on the mechanics of Mechner's video game, Dastan excels in extraordinary leaps and jumps, converted into believable cinematic terms by a stunt team that included David Belle, the French founder of parkour—a discipline somewhere between acrobatics and martial arts that utilizes any means necessary in getting from point A to point B.

Chosen to star opposite Gyllenhaal as the beautiful and haughty Princess Tamina was a young British actress whose career was just beginning to blossom: Gemma Arterton, a recent graduate of the Royal Academy of Dramatic Art. Bruckheimer and Newell then surrounded his attractive young leads with a richly talented cast that included mostly British actors, including Sir Ben Kingsley, Alfred Molina, Richard Coyle, and Toby Kebbell. The action and romance were set against spectacular sets by production designer Wolf Kroeger, dramatic landscapes in Morocco, and on nine Pinewood Studios soundstages outside London.

The film emerged as a worthy successor to the Pirates of the Caribbean and National Treasure movies, as well as such classic Walt Disney-produced, live-action period adventures as *Treasure Island*, *The Sword and the Rose*, *Swiss Family Robinson*, and *The Fighting Prince of Donegal*. *Prince of Persia* was imbued with a rich storybook-come-to-life quality through its lustrous, color-saturated imagery and fairy-tale–like story. The filmmakers also worked in clever nods to boy's-own-adventure movies of the past, and these allusions were well appreciated by respected critic and film scholar Richard Corliss. In *Time* magazine, Corliss published a highly appreciative précis of the film, putting it into the context of what he had perceived to be a dreary start of the summer at the cinema:

"Could this be the summer when big movies run out of steam, scope, and pizzazz? Not if Jerry Bruckheimer has his say . . . the first Pirates, in 2003, was a zesty surprise. His new *Prince of Persia: The Sands of Time* . . . is another. Just as the swashbuckling heroes of Douglas Fairbanks and Errol Flynn sagas did, *Persia*'s Dastan (Jake Gyllenhaal) arrives in the nick of time to save the industry's imperiled faith in May megamovies . . . it scampers through the history of Hollywood adventure, filching every Saturday-matinee touchstone, from Indiana Jones to Chuck Jones's 1957 cartoon *Ali Baba Bunny* . . ."

Released just before Memorial Day, *Prince of Persia: The Sands of Time* was only the first of Bruckheimer's tent-pole Disney films debuting in the summer of 2010; in mid-July the studio released *The Sorcerer's Apprentice*. This project reunited Bruckheimer with Nicolas Cage (for the seventh time) and *National Treasure* and *National Treasure: Book of Secrets* director Jon Turteltaub (for the third time). The idea for the film originated with Cage—a great fan of Disneyana—who proposed to tell a contemporary story of magic and sorcery set in modern-day Manhattan. Cage was inspired by the immortal episode of Walt Disney's 1940 *Fantasia* starring Mickey Mouse, which was itself based on both the original 1797 poem ("Der Zauberlehrling") by Johann Wolfgang von Goethe, and the Paul Dukas musical tone poem first performed a hundred years thereafter.

The protagonist, Balthazar Blake (Cage), is a 1,000-year-old sorcerer who was a student of Merlin himself. When Merlin is murdered by Morgana le Fay, Blake embarks on a search through the centuries for the Prime Merlinean, the inheritor of Merlin's power. The unlikely candidate uncovered for this heralded position is Dave Stutler (Jay Baruchel), a nerdy physics major at New York University whose world is turned upside down by Balthazar. The script by Matt Lopez, Doug Miro, and Carlo Bernard posits interesting questions of where magic and science depart and where they intersect, all the while entertaining the audience with adventure, fantasy, and romance, set against a New York City landscape that often literally springs to life thanks to visual effects supervisor John Nelson and his team.

"I love the world of magic, and to be able to bring that to a contemporary audience was really appealing to me," says Bruckheimer. "I've always liked stories that have a magical element, and *The Sorcerer's Apprentice* is one of the great magical stories of all time. We thought it would be tremendously exciting to develop the core of that concept into a brand-new story set in the modern world."

Three of the actors enlisted to work with Cage on-screen were already well known to Bruckheimer. Jay Baruchel, the fast-rising, young Canadian-born talent, had already starred in the Bruckheimer-produced TV series *Just Legal* opposite Don Johnson as an underage prodigy lawyer. And both Alfred Molina and Toby Kebbell had so impressed Bruckheimer with their performances in *Prince of Persia: The Sands of Time*, that the producer recommended them to Turteltaub to portray, respectively, Maxim Horvath and fellow Morganian Drake Stone. Teresa Palmer, a fresh and appealing newcomer from Australia, was cast as Dave Stutler's elusive object of desire from childhood, and Italian beauty Monica Bellucci was cast as Veronica, who is beloved by both Balthazar and Horvath

through the centuries. The film utilized numerous New York City locations, as well as spectacular sets from production designer Naomi Shohan. The audience got an added kick of magic and fun when such landmarks as the Chrysler Building's eagle gargoyles and the Charging Bull sculpture in the Wall Street area literally came to life in the course of the story.

Once again, Bruckheimer, Cage, and Turteltaub had collaborated on a film that, like the National Treasure entries, sought to charm and entertain in equal measure, with the added attraction of spectacular displays of sorcery and magic. "We've tried very hard with *The Sorcerer's Apprentice* to honor those past wizards—Goethe, Dukas, and especially Walt Disney—while at the same time finding a magic of our own to weave around the audience," notes Bruckheimer. "It's quite a mandate, and one that we all took very seriously."

Next up for Bruckheimer was the fourth entry in the Pirates of the Caribbean series, this one subtitled *On Stranger Tides*. Filming began in June 2010, priming the films' rabid fans for more of what they had already experienced in the first three movies and then some, thanks to a new director (Rob Marshall) and fresh cast additions (such as Penélope Cruz, Ian McShane, Sam Claflin, and Astrid Bergès-Frisbey).

For Jerry Bruckheimer, as always, it's about doing everything possible to satisfy expectations. "We do everything we can to make great entertainment, but ultimately, it's the moviegoer's decision. And what was true in my father's business is the same as the movie business . . . the customer's always right!"

CON AIR

PAGE 111, TOP LEFT:
Jerry and Linda Bruckheimer chat on the set of Con Air, *while director Simon West takes a cell phone call.*

Page 111, MIDDLE LEFT:
Con Air *director Simon West.*

PAGE 111, BOTTOM, SECOND FROM RIGHT:
John Cusack with Jerry Bruckheimer on set.

Jerry Bruckheimer chats with Nicolas Cage on the Con Air *set, beginning a long and fruitful creative association.*

ARMAGEDDON

ENEMY OF THE STATE

GONE IN SIXTY SECONDS

COYOTE UGLY

REMEMBER THE TITANS

PEARL HARBOR

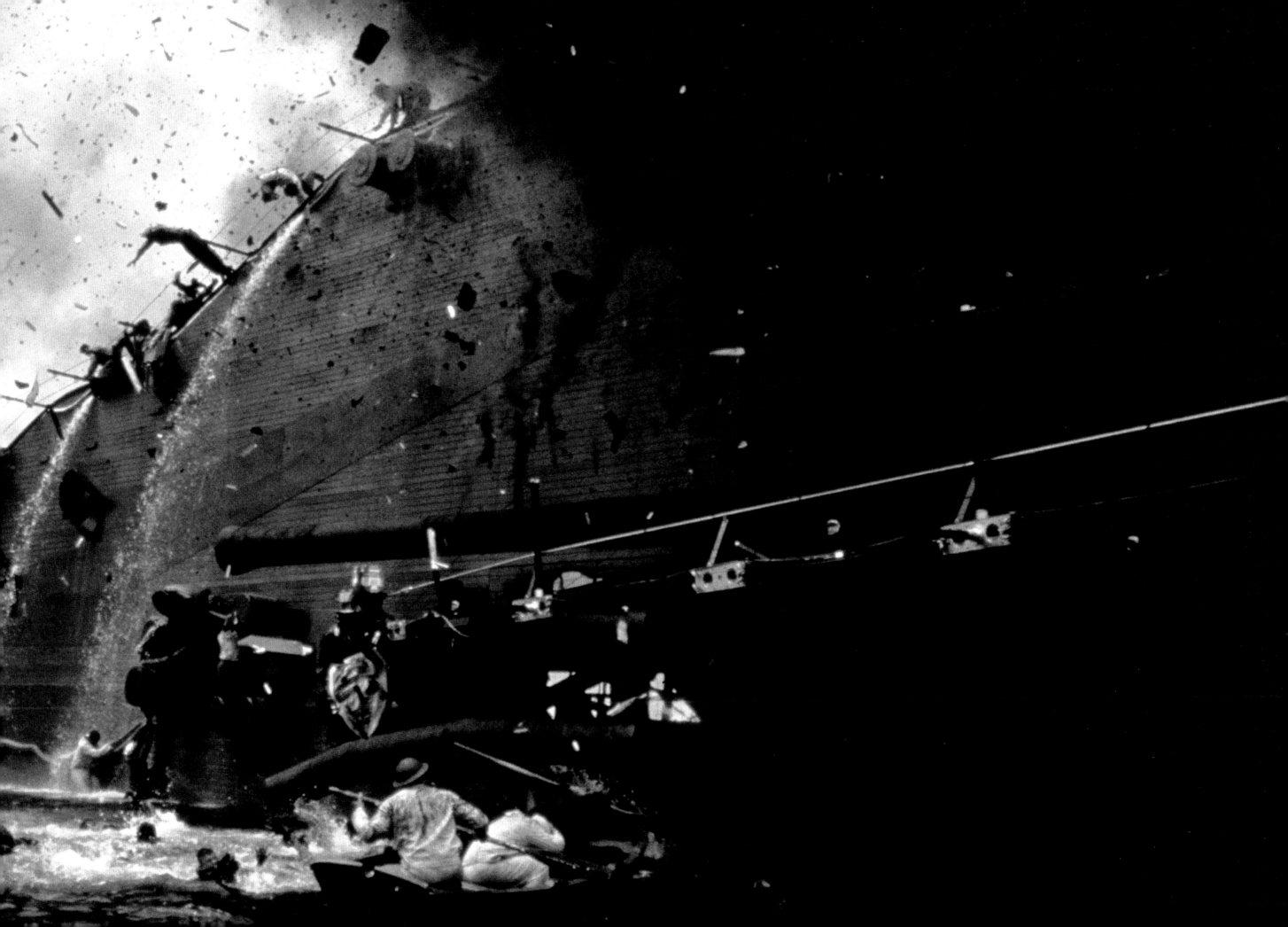

BLACK HAWK DOWN

PAGE 146, TOP LEFT:
Jerry Bruckheimer and director Ridley Scott on
the Rabat, Morocco, location of Black Hawk Down.

PAGE 151, BOTTOM RIGHT:
Jerry Bruckheimer chats with
Chris Rock on the Bad Company set.

BAD COMPANY

KANGAROO JACK

VERONICA GUERIN

TOP RIGHT:
Director Joel Schumacher and Jerry Bruckheimer on the Irish location of Veronica Guerin.

BOTTOM RIGHT:
Cate Blanchett chats on the Veronica Guerin *set with director Joel Schumacher and Colin Farrell, who made a cameo appearance in the film.*

KING ARTHUR

GLORY ROAD

Jerry Bruckheimer chats on the Glory Road set with director James Gartner.

DÉJÀ VU

Director Tony Scott, in his signature pink baseball cap, directs Denzel Washington in Déjà Vu.

CONFESSIONS OF A SHOPAHOLIC

Director P. J. Hogan and Jerry Bruckheimer with Executive
Producer Mike Stenson and author Madeleine Wickham
watch the replay of a camera setup on the Confessions of
a Shopaholic set.

Author Madeleine Wickham (who writes the Shopaholic novels under the pen name
Sophie Kinsella), Executive Producer Chad Oman, Jerry Bruckheimer, and
Bruckheimer Films Executive Vice President of production Melissa Reid on the
Confessions of a Shopaholic set on the first day of filming in Connecticut.

PAGE 171, BOTTOM RIGHT:
Jerry Bruckheimer shares a smile with director

G-FORCE

PRINCE OF PERSIA: SANDS OF TIME

TOP LEFT: Property master David Balfour displays the "hero" Dagger of Time to Jerry Bruckheimer and Executive Producer Chad Oman in the Morocco location where Prince of Persia: The Sands of Time *was being shot.*

BOTTOM LEFT: Director Mike Newell points out a key moment on the replay monitor to the amusement of star Jake Gyllenhaal on the Prince of Persia: The Sands of Time *set.*

THE SORCERER'S APPRENTICE

THE BRUCKHEIMER FRANCHISES:
COPS, BAD BOYS, NATIONAL TREASURES, AND ESPECIALLY PIRATES

"Some people think that franchise just means dollar signs," observes Jerry Bruckheimer, "but to me it means that people liked a world you've created enough to want to go back to it." It's worthy to note that none of the franchises that have emanated from Bruckheimer's cinematic workshop were ever designed that way from the start. "I would never be arrogant enough to assume before a film has even opened that the public would automatically want more," the producer continues. "Every one of our movies has been a stand-alone. But if audiences respond enthusiastically enough, and the characters and stories can be further developed, then it's great to bring them back for other adventures."

The Bruckheimer franchises haven't only been limited to the big screen. The CSI television franchise, which now includes *CSI: Crime Scene Investigation* (the first one to air), *CSI: Miami*, and *CSI: NY*, are three of the most successful series in the history of the medium.

BEVERLY HILLS COP: THE EDDIE MURPHY ROCKETSHIP

Beverly Hills Cop (1984), the first of Bruckheimer's films to emerge as a bona fide franchise, had so many initial casting problems that its ultimate success is even more impressive. It's a classic fish-out-of-water story about a brash and streetwise Detroit policeman, Axel Foley, who follows the trail of a friend's murder to Beverly Hills. Rising young star Mickey Rourke was originally cast, but script delays and his commitment to another role took him out of the picture. Sylvester Stallone then came aboard, but he parted ways with the producers when his rewrites of Dan Petrie, Jr.'s screenplay didn't align with their vision of the project. A stroke of casting genius then occurred when Bruckheimer and Simpson offered the title role to the twenty-three-year-old phenomenon Eddie Murphy, then under exclusive contract to Paramount. His involvement helped to convert what might have been an entertaining but routine action film into an outrageous comedic romp.

Simpson, and especially Bruckheimer, fought hard for their offbeat choice of director, Martin Brest, whose only previous feature was the quirky senior-citizen caper comedy *Going in Style* with George Burns, Art Carney, and Lee Strasberg. Bruckheimer had to convince not only Paramount, but Brest himself, who finally agreed to let the decision lay on the flip of a coin. "I was scared to look," Brest recalled to *New York Times* writer Lindsey Gruson in a December 1984 story about the making of the film. "But I had made a firm commitment to adhere to the outcome. It came up heads, so I said I'd do it." This story is illustrative not only of Bruckheimer's tenacity, but his career-long insistence on casting against type, regardless of whether it's tapping actors or directors.

Axel Foley's status as a working-class hero made him a lightning rod for mass audiences, particularly insofar as the villain of the piece, Victor Maitland (Steven Berkoff), was a rich and respected member of the community. Brest's strength with actors and character was particularly seen in his supporting players, including Judge Reinhold and John Ashton, who, as Beverly Hills detectives Rosewood and Taggart, wind up assisting Axel in his search for justice. Also supporting Murphy was Bronson Pinchot in his now-classic depiction of Serge, an effete art-gallery clerk of indeterminate (and possibly fake) foreign extraction.

Released for Christmas 1984, *Beverly Hills Cop* was a smash hit around the world, and the number-one film of the year with worldwide grosses of $316 million, remarkable for an R-rated film. Adjusted to contemporary numbers, this totals nearly $700 million, which gives a more accurate representation of its phenomenal success. Ultimately, it was a film that helped to boost nearly everyone involved on the Hollywood map, from Jerry Bruckheimer and Don Simpson to director Martin Brest, and on to nearly everyone in the cast, especially its brash, dynamic star, Eddie Murphy.

Beverly Hills Cop II (1987) was the inevitable follow-up to the hit comedy-action film, with Eddie Murphy returning as Axel Foley, along with supporting players Judge Reinhold, Ronny Cox, and John Ashton. This time, Simpson and Bruckheimer called upon the directorial skills of Tony Scott, in his first outing for the pair since *Top Gun*. "We were originally going to take Axel to London," recalls Bruckheimer, "but then realized that a movie called *Beverly Hills Cop* shouldn't take place out of the country, let alone out of Southern California."

In the second film, Foley, who's back at work in Detroit, is asked to return to Beverly Hills by detectives Rosewood and Taggart (Reinhold and Ashton, respectively) to help them with a case after their captain (Cox's character) has been targeted and badly wounded by a shooter. The culprits turn out to be a group of wealthy people who are committing

a series of high-profile break-ins that are dubbed the "Alphabet Crimes," robberies at heavily guarded, prime locations. Once again, the crimes accentuated the class differences that informed the first movie.

Just like the first film, *Beverly Hills Cop II* featured a balance between Murphy's manic humor and hard action, and it paid off. The film grossed nearly as much as the first, with worldwide revenue totals that were just $40,000 shy of $300 million.

BAD BOYS: BRUCKHEIMER, BAY, SMITH, AND LAWRENCE

Bruckheimer's second franchise would also offer audiences a policier that didn't stint on either the thrills or the laughs, and this one would introduce a new director to the ranks of feature filmmakers: a tall, lanky, preternaturally energetic thirty-year-old named Michael Bay.

"Michael and I were good friends since even before *Bad Boys*," Bruckheimer told *Fade In*'s Dan Cox in 1998. "He did a very good video for us for *Days of Thunder*. I looked at his work—in fact, he'd only done a couple of videos at that point—and just saw how talented he was. And then, when *Bad Boys* came around a few years later, I looked at his work again and saw how he'd grown as an artist, how he'd matured.

"I believe Michael is the next generation of big-event filmmakers," the producer continued, foretelling the success that Bay would have both in association with Bruckheimer and on his own with the Transformers franchise. "I believe he's the next guy that's going to fill that niche."

Bruckheimer's comments, and faith in Bay, were certainly precognitive, as the young director would indeed fulfill all of the producer's expectations—first in collaboration with

Bruckheimer on *Bad Boys*, *The Rock*, *Armageddon*, *Pearl Harbor*, and *Bad Boys II*; and then with Steven Spielberg on the three Transformers action spectaculars, confirming the trust and faith that Bruckheimer demonstrated in giving him his first crack at feature filmmaking.

Bad Boys had been in development since the Simpson and Bruckheimer days at Paramount, and it was originally written with *Saturday Night Live* comedic actors Dana Carvey and Jon Lovitz in mind. Just as *Beverly Hills Cop* underwent a major tectonic shift when the role passed from Sylvester Stallone to Eddie Murphy, so did *Bad Boys* evolve when the roles of Miami-Dade narcotics detectives Marcus Burnett and Mike Lowrey were offered to Martin Lawrence and Will Smith. Will Smith was already a big recording artist and television star, starting in the late 1980s under his rap-de-plume The Fresh Prince, followed by the long-running TV comedy *The Fresh Prince of Bel-Air*. But with *Bad Boys*, the charismatic young Smith was about to get a mighty career boost. "I had met Will, thought he could be a movie star, and gave him the *Bad Boys* script," recalls Bruckheimer. "Columbia actually wanted Arsenio Hall for that role, but he passed."

Martin Lawrence, like Will, was a big TV star at the time, also top-lining his own show, *Martin*. "Don and I never gave up," Bruckheimer told *Hollywood Reporter* columnist Martin Grove. "We had the thought to put Martin Lawrence in the picture. Martin read the script and flipped over it, and wanted to do it. Will Smith is somebody [whose career] Don and I have followed—first his music career, then his television career, and his acting career—and we felt it would be a great comedy-cop-buddy movie." The producers would know, having pioneered the genre with the first two Beverly Hills Cop entries. Following Gere, Cruise, and Murphy before them, Lawrence and Smith were to become major movie stars with their first Bruckheimer film.

Bad Boys, which premiered in 1995, was moderately budgeted, but Bay seemed to stretch the money with bold on-screen action, including the requisite killer car chases and gunplay. "Michael was so determined to get bang for the buck," recalls Bruckheimer, "that he actually put in his own money to shoot a scene." Audiences responded to Bay and the film's take-no-prisoners approach to the tune of $141 million internationally, bringing a very healthy profit to a project that only cost approximately $19 million.

Although the first film brought in a very decent return, the $65 million domestic take did not necessarily demand a sequel. "The first *Bad Boys* wasn't a huge success," admits Bruckheimer, "[though] not bad for a $20 million movie. But what happened was video and DVD. The movie began selling through the roof and took on a whole new life. Suddenly, there was demand for a sequel."

Bad Boys II (2003) followed nearly a decade after the original's release, so it was a long time coming for the film's fans. Michael Bay returned to the director's chair, and Martin Lawrence and Will Smith reprised their roles as Burnett and Lowrey. With a bigger budget and more ambitious canvas, Bruckheimer (now producing solo after Simpson's passing) and Bay ramped up the action and mayhem quotient as the streetwise heroes tangle with a Cuban drug lord, the Russian Mafia, and Haitian gangs.

The chemistry between Smith (who had become a massive star in the years between the first and second Bad Boys films) and Lawrence was in full effect, due in large part, according to the producer, to their commitment to the work, and to each other. "They were so generous," Bruckheimer told TV journalist Charlie Rose in a 2003 interview. "Every Sunday, we'd go through the week's work, we'd rehearse everything, and Will would come in

and say, 'I found these great lines for Martin,' and Martin would come in and say, 'Will should say this.' That's the kind of giving and sharing that makes hit movies."

While no one would describe *Bad Boys II* as a "critic's movie," it certainly won over some key reviewers. "Plot, schmot. *Bad Boys II* is an unabashed guilty pleasure," headlined Ellen A. Kim's take in the *Seattle Post-Intelligencer*, who noted, ". . . watching a Bruckheimer with natural comics like Smith and Lawrence makes it all go down easily . . ."

In *The Boston Globe*, Wesley Morris proffered that, "Bay's movie is . . . a confident megaproduction that feels it doesn't need to lean on the visual frills if it has Smith and Lawrence—it's a natural-born buddy flick." Audiences didn't care if it was a "guilty pleasure" or not. *Bad Boys II* amassed $138 million domestically, more than doubling the first film's take, with a $273 million international total.

PIRATES OF THE CARIBBEAN: MAKING MOVIE HISTORY

The year 2003 also saw the dawn of Jerry Bruckheimer's most successful franchise. But more than that, it was a game-changing, culture-altering, zeitgeist-boosting, history-making phenomenon: *Pirates of the Caribbean*. It may be hard to believe now—especially considering that a month after the release of *On Stranger Tides* in 2011, three of the four Pirates films ranked in the list of top-ten grossing films of all time—but the project had cards stacked against it from inception. "A pirate movie in 2003?" questions Bruckheimer rhetorically. "Ridiculous! The genre was completely and officially dead and buried. No major pirate film had been made since the mid-1990s, and that was a disaster. So was the one before that in the eighties. And the one before that in the seventies. Three

decades, three strikes. And a movie based on a Disneyland ride? You should have seen all of the raised eyebrows."

In art, as in life, history has a strange way of coming full circle. The evidence? The first on-screen image ever to appear in an all live-action Walt Disney Studios feature was none other than a close-up of the skull and crossbones Jolly Roger flag in the classic 1950 version of Robert Louis Stevenson's *Treasure Island*.

Some fifty-three years later, the same skull and crossbones would grace the screen when the very same studio's *Pirates of the Caribbean: The Curse of the Black Pearl* spectacularly reinvented and reinvigorated a moribund genre. From childhood classics like *Treasure Island* and Howard Pyle's *Book of Pirates*, to a long run of classic films, such as *The Black Pirate*, *The Crimson Pirate*, and *The Buccaneer*, swashbuckling tales of high-seas derring-do, both nefarious and noble, were seemingly never-ending and always a hit—in their day.

Alas, as far as filmmakers in this century were concerned, pirates were forgotten as subjects worthy of contemporary moviemaking. That is, until Jerry Bruckheimer, his chosen director, Gore Verbinski, and a brilliant company of actors and behind-the-scenes artists breathed new life into the genre's sails, inspired by the Disney attraction that has delighted generations since its 1967 debut at Disneyland in Anaheim. The Pirates of the Caribbean ride, which utilized the then brand-new technology of Audio-Animatronics that Walt Disney and his Imagineers developed, soon became a major part of pop culture, with its cheery refrains of, "Yo ho yo ho, a pirate's life for me" (and the less cheery warning that, "Dead men tell no tales"), sung and quoted by millions.

The Pirates movie saga began back in 1992, when screenwriters Ted Elliott and Terry Rossio—who had just enjoyed a major success cowriting Walt Disney Studios'

Aladdin—pitched a film version of the Pirates of the Caribbean attraction to production executives. Considering the fact that all recent pirate films had sailed out of port only to wind up dead in the water, it's not surprising that the studio chose to pass. Eight years later, in the spring of 2000, Walt Disney Studios reconsidered the notion of converting the attraction into a feature film. In light of his recent success having written the excellent retro-swashbuckler *The Count of Monte Cristo* for the studio's Touchstone Pictures, Disney called upon the screenwriting talents of Jay Wolpert. His efforts were then bolstered by Stuart Beattie, one of the writers of the taut thriller *Collateral*.

But when Dick Cook, then chairman of The Walt Disney Studios, first approached Bruckheimer about the project, the producer's response was not altogether encouraging. "I thought about it and said I didn't want to make a movie based on an attraction, that it really didn't interest me. But I read the script and felt although it was too linear, too expensive, and lacked the pizzazz that I like to give to an audience, there were possibilities."

Poetic justice was achieved when Bruckheimer asked none other than Ted Elliott and Terry Rossio to take a crack at the material. "Ted and Terry are wonderful writers who came in with an element of the movie that really excited me—the supernatural," notes Bruckheimer. "It was Ted and Terry who took the supernatural element of the ride and applied it to the story, creating the idea of cursed pirates, which was the little edge that made me think this was something really special. I thought audiences could be reintroduced to the pirate genre if they were given something new, exciting, spectacular, and original."

After more than a decade of languishing, *Pirates of the Caribbean* was finally up and running as a major feature-film project. Elliott and Rossio were also determined to

utilize elements of the Pirates of the Caribbean attraction in their screen story, as both were longtime fans. The story of what finally emerged as *Pirates of the Caribbean: The Curse of the Black Pearl* went through the usual metamorphoses that are an integral part of the Hollywood process. In the original story composed by Disney executive Brigham Taylor, creative executive Michael Haines, and Josh Harmon, of the studio's story department, Will, a prison guard, sets out to rescue Elizabeth, the governor's daughter, when she's kidnapped and held for ransom by a pirate named Blackheart. In order to save her, Will must link fortunes with Jack, a former member of Blackheart's pirate crew.

This version was further developed and refined by Jay Wolpert, who introduced some real-life pirate figures in cameo appearances. Stuart Beattie added the characters of Commodore Norrington (replacing a villainous Captain of the Guard named Defoe in the original story), Captain Wraith (replacing Blackheart), and the ornithological surnames of Elizabeth and Jack: Swann and Sparrow.

But it was Elliott and Rossio, who at Bruckheimer's urging, laced the story with supernatural elements, such as the notion of the cursed Aztec gold and what it's done to the *Black Pearl* and her unfortunate crew of the living dead. Elliott and Rossio, also replaced Captain Wraith/ Blackheart with a new character named Barbossa, inserted several intentional moments that directly reflected the Pirates attraction, and, while retaining the romantic flourishes of the previous drafts, refined and polished the story until it positively gleamed with possibilities for truly original big-screen entertainment.

Bruckheimer found his director in Gore Verbinski, again a young veteran of television commercials, who had already made his mark as a dazzlingly original visual and dramatic stylist on such features as *Mouse*

Hunt and *The Mexican*. He had also directed *The Ring*, which at that point had not yet been released.

At the same time, Elliott and Rossio were still shaping and forming—on the written page, anyway—the character of Captain Jack Sparrow. When Elliott and Rossio first presented Gore Verbinski with their take on the tale, the director was enthusiastic. But it would be a twist of fate, and another unusual casting choice, that would truly bring Captain Jack to life in all his swaggering, wonderful glory. Johnny Depp, an actor known more for his offbeat, deeply personal performances than for action heroics or swashbuckling, was being avidly pursued by Bruckheimer and Verbinski for the role. Once again, Bruckheimer was determined to go against conventional casting expectations. "I flew to France twice to see Johnny [Depp]," recalls Bruckheimer, "and we had a three- or four-hour lunch where I tried to convince him to do the movie."

Thankfully, Depp decided to embark on the voyage, although it almost didn't leave the dock. Ironically, the film that was to become a legend and launch one of the most successful franchises of all time almost wasn't made. "The plug was pulled twice because of budget issues," recalls Jerry Bruckheimer Films president Mike Stenson. "There was about a ten-to-fifteen-million-dollar variance between us and the studio, but in the end there was compromise on both sides and we got the green light. It's always challenging when you have a large-scale film with plenty of shooting on water and visual effects." Temporary shutdowns are a common occurrence in the feature film world, and *Pirates of the Caribbean: The Curse of the Black Pearl* was neither the first nor last movie that would require Bruckheimer to call upon his skills of diplomacy and negotiation to get a project back on track. *Pearl Harbor* had experienced such a shutdown three years previously, and, as was well chronicled in the media, *The Lone Ranger* would also go through such a process eight years later.

But the film that emerged, *Pirates of the Caribbean: The Curse of the Black Pearl*, was a true anomaly—an adventure/comedy/fantasy/swashbuckler that melted one genre into another with alarming ease, creating enduring characters, including at least one, Captain Jack Sparrow, who became the first truly iconic screen character of the new millennium. Depp was joined by a marvelous cast, including Australian-born Oscar winner Geoffrey Rush as Captain Barbossa, Orlando Bloom as Will Turner, Keira Knightley as Elizabeth Swann, and Jack Davenport as Norrington. *The Curse of the Black Pearl* created a new Pirates world that lived by its own duplicitous rules, much to the delight of the audience. For locations, Verbinski took his huge company to undiscovered regions of St. Vincent and the Grenadines in the heart of the West Indies, as well as Los Angeles, for studio and other location work.

The story of cursed pirates who become skeletons by moonlight pulled a clever switch on the usual swashbuckler story insofar as a treasure had to be returned rather than taken to end their affliction. Using the ride as a springboard, with clever references to the attraction's content sprinkled throughout, *Pirates of the Caribbean: The Curse of the Black Pearl* defied some less-than-enthusiastic anticipation for a "movie based on a ride" and became a smash hit everywhere it played. After opening on July 9, 2003, it ultimately amassed a domestic U.S. gross of $305,413,918 and, including its record-breaking overseas engagements, a worldwide total of $653,913,918. The film also received five Academy Award nominations, including Best Actor for Johnny Depp.

Critics were quite effusive in their praise. "All in all, *Pirates of the Caribbean* is the best spectacle of the summer,"

wrote David Denby in *The New Yorker*. "The absence of pomp is a relief, the warmth of the comedy a pleasure."

"This is an original work in an antique mood," added Richard Corliss in *Time*. "The actors and authors all have fun with the genre without making fun of it. Rather, they revive it."

"Finally," wrote Claudia Puig in *USA Today*, "there's a big-budget popcorn movie that delivers what moviegoers hunger for: humor, action, thrills, and charismatic characters. *Pirates of the Caribbean: The Curse of the Black Pearl* is the summer blockbuster we've been waiting for."

While rooted in the fundamentals of classic Disney family films, *The Curse of the Black Pearl* proved that a "family film" could find a wholly contemporary groove, and spin with it till the wheels fell off.

The irony is that the initial dailies emanating from the shoot succeeded in veritably freaking out some of the Disney studio heads who didn't know what to make of Johnny Depp's utterly unconventional, even subversive, interpretation of a piratical antihero. Bruckheimer, however, stood behind his star and director. "We already knew it played because we had a read-through, and it was very funny," Bruckheimer told *Variety*'s Ben Fritz in 2006. "Dailies are dailies, and you can be incredibly flamboyant as long as you have those moments of reality. I told the studio, 'If you're really worried, I'll cut a scene together and show you a realistic cut.' I essentially said, 'You guys hired him because of his brilliant interpretations of characters. You can get any guy to play it straight.'" Obviously, Bruckheimer's faith was amply rewarded a billion times over and further confirmed by Depp's Academy Award and Golden Globe nominations.

Clearly, there was an international mandate for more Pirates, and Jerry Bruckheimer and Gore Verbinski, along with Walt Disney Pictures, decided that just one sequel

would not be enough. It made practical sense, economically, to film two follow-ups simultaneously, taking full advantage of locations, sets, and the availability of its increasingly in-demand stars. It also made sense creatively, because with the characters so well established in the first film, taking them on further voyages was an exciting prospect.

When the time came for the filmmakers to tackle *Pirates of the Caribbean: Dead Man's Chest* and *Pirates of the Caribbean: At World's End*, Bruckheimer, Verbinski, Elliott, and Rossio all knew what they didn't want to do: repeat themselves. "We were hoping for the success of *The Curse of the Black Pearl* so that we could make more Pirates movies," notes Bruckheimer, "and we wanted everything in the second and third films to relate back to what started everything off in the first."

Dead Man's Chest introduced the astonishing creation of the octopus-bearded Davy Jones, with British actor Bill Nighy providing the movements, voice, and soul for what was then fully digitized with extraordinary photo-realism by visual effects supervisor John Knoll of ILM and his team of wizards. Knoll utilized brand-new motion capture technologies, and was rewarded for his efforts with an Academy Award (which he shared with Hal T. Hickel, Charles Gibson, and Allen Hall). Taking the supernatural thread several steps further, *Dead Man's Chest* dipped even more deeply into the treasure trove of pirate and seagoing lore and mythology than the living skeletons of *The Curse of the Black Pearl*, including the legendary Kraken, a sea monster fabled since twelfth-century Norwegian chronicles.

Several new characters were added in *Dead Man's Chest* and *At World's End*, along with Davy Jones, including Will's accursed father, "Bootstrap Bill" Turner (Stellan Skarsgard); Chinese corsair, Captain Sao Feng (Chow Yun-Fat); Caribbean soothsayer Tia Dalma (Naomie Harris); the ruthless Lord Cutler Beckett (Tom Hollander) of the East India Trading Company (representing the corporate crushing of free enterprise as embodied by pirates); Beckett's enforcer, Mercer (David Schofield); and even immortal Rolling Stones guitarist Keith Richards, a close friend of Johnny Depp's and acknowledged by the actor as an inspiration for Sparrow's physical and vocal characteristics, as Captain Jack's father, Captain Teague, keeper of the Pirata Codex (Pirate Code) itself.

The marathon 284-day combined shoot of *Dead Man's Chest* and *At World's End* took the company back to St. Vincent in the West Indies, as well as the gorgeously underdeveloped island of Dominica, Grand Bahama Island (where Hurricane Wilma forced the company to evacuate and destroyed several sets in October 2005), and the Exumas (a part of the Bahamas). The company then headed back to the U.S. for studio and location work in the Los Angeles and Central Coast areas of California, out to the Bonneville Salt Flats in Utah for scenes in Davy Jones' Locker, and finally to the Hawaiian islands of Maui and Molokai.

The proof of how greatly the Pirates franchise had exploded in the national consciousness was in the box office till. Not even Bruckheimer or Verbinski, nor Walt Disney Studios, could have predicted what would happen when the second film in the trilogy, *Pirates of the Caribbean: Dead Man's Chest*, opened on July 7, 2006. The zeitgeist is a mysterious entity, and Pirates had obviously plugged directly into its circuit board, as *Dead Man's Chest* became an instant cultural phenomenon. Upon its opening three-day weekend, *Dead Man's Chest* blew every preceding U.S. box office record apart, amassing an astonishing $135,745,219, surpassing the previous champ, 2002's *Spider-Man*, by more than $20 million.

"Big Booty for Bruckaneers," screamed a headline of the Hollywood trade paper *Daily Variety* in its unique parlance, pointing out that the three-day numbers even beat the standing four-day weekend record . . . that the Friday totals of $55.5 million set a new mark for the biggest one-day numbers ever . . . that by Saturday, its $100.2 million take was the biggest ever two-day gross, which meant that *Dead Man's Chest* was the first movie in history to break the sacred $100 million mark in forty-eight hours. By this point, the film had taken on major-event status, as evidenced by the legion of Pirates fans sweeping across the demographic board, who lined up for hours, many sporting an array of buccaneer gear, some so comprehensively attired from head to toe that it looked as if they had stepped right off the set.

By the end of its second weekend, *Dead Man's Chest* had passed $200 million on its eighth day of release—another record sent crashing to the ground—and amassed $258.2 million in only ten days, bringing in an additional $125 million in twenty-four countries outside of the U.S. and Canada, while 65 percent of markets had yet to open. Any lingering doubts about the Pirates' sea "legs" were laid to rest after the third weekend of *Dead Man's Chest*, in which the film soared past four major new releases and became the fastest film in history to pass the $300 million mark in the U.S. and Canada (and broke *The Curse of the Black Pearl*'s $305 million milepost). And overseas, opening in eleven new markets, it was the same story over and over again: number one everywhere. Crumbling records. Long queues from Tokyo to Mumbai to Warsaw, and back again. Final worldwide tally: an astounding $1.1 billion!

With the filmmakers taking considerable chances with the film's ambitiousness, many critics, like *Rolling Stone*'s Peter Travers, appreciated the effort. "The second Pirates does more than improve on the original, it pumps out the bilge

and offers a fresh start. Returning director Gore Verbinski and screenwriters Terry Rossio and Ted Elliott have wisely taken a cue from Depp and learned how to play fast and loose with the material. Live is an odd word for something called *Dead Man's Chest*, but lively it is. You won't find hotter action, wilder thrills, or loopier laughs this summer."

For *At World's End*, Verbinski, Elliott, and Rossio pushed themselves even further—quite literally, to the ends of the earth, depicting Davy Jones' Locker in a manner that resulted in some of the most surreal sequences ever seen in a mainstream, big-audience movie. The two-hour-and-thirty-eight-minute running time, complex plot figure eights, and a multitude of characters thrilled many fans and confounded others, but resulted in a film loaded with breakthrough sequences. Most notable of these incredible scenes was the climactic "Maelstrom" battle, which contained some of the most complex visual-effects shots ever composed.

Critics had strong opinions on the merits of *At World's End*, a film of nearly overwhelming ambition and a degree of experimentation rare in studio projects. "Exciting, distracting, and quite possibly permanently concentration impairing, what *Pirates of the Caribbean: At World's End* offers is a wonderfully scenic medley of impressive action sequences so lengthy, elaborate, and numerous that remembering what came before becomes a kind of test of mental focus," noted Carina Chocano in the *Los Angeles Times*.

At World's End added yet another $960 million worldwide to the franchise's treasure chest that by now had amassed $2.7 billion—and that's a lot of booty. Despite the lack of any new Pirates films between 2007 and 2011, the mania showed no sign of abating. Pseudo-Captain Jack Sparrows popped up everywhere, usually seen taking photos with tourists for dollars, trick-or-treating for Halloween, walking around the Disney theme parks (either officially costumed or devotees donning the colors as die-hard fans), or on the ubiquitous "Talk Like a Pirate Days" that suddenly sprang up all over the world. And when Britain's *Total Film* magazine issued a special edition entitled "Top 100 Movie Characters of All Time," as voted by their readers, the number-one position went to someone who beat out the likes of Stanley Kowalski, Mrs. Robinson, The Man with No Name, HAL 9000, Frankenstein's monster, Dracula, Charles Foster Kane, E.T., Rocky Balboa, Scarlett O'Hara, Travis Bickle, Indiana Jones, and Darth Vader: Captain Jack Sparrow!

It was inevitable, given the unprecedented success of the trilogy, that more Pirates would follow. When the time came to prepare a fourth entry in the series—to be titled *Pirates of the Caribbean: On Stranger Tides*—Jerry Bruckheimer and the team of Elliott and Rossio began collaborating on the story from the earliest stages with Johnny Depp himself. But when the bell rang out to signify the start of a new watch, one crew member did not come up on deck. Having expended incredible amounts of time, energy, and creativity on his Pirates films, director Gore Verbinski moved on to other projects.

Bringing in his own stylish sensibilities to the franchise was Rob Marshall, whose very first directorial outing, *Chicago*, had won six Academy Awards, including one for Best Picture of the Year. "Rob started as a dancer and choreographer, and understands action and movement," observed Bruckheimer before filming began in 2010. "Then he became a brilliant director who understands humor and drama. I think people love to be entertained, love to laugh, and love to be frightened, and that's what we want to give them again in *On Stranger Tides*, with a fresh cast joining familiar faces."

Partially utilizing Tim Powers's highly regarded 1988 cult novel *On Stranger Tides* as source material (although effectively merged by Elliott and Rossio into the Pirates

of the Caribbean universe), the film picked up almost exactly where *At World's End* left off, with Captain Jack in possession of a map (stolen from Barbossa) to the legendary Fountain of Youth. On the journey that follows, he not only encounters the equally legendary Blackbeard (Ian McShane), "the pirate that all other pirates fear," but also a flame from his past, Angelica (Penélope Cruz, another Academy Award winner), who may or may not be Blackbeard's daughter. The voyage indeed takes them on stranger tides, introducing zombie pirates and voracious mermaids, continuing the supernatural thread so crucial to the success of the franchise. Other new cast additions included the up-and-coming young British actor Sam Claflin as Philip, an earnest, young missionary, and the ethereally beautiful French-Spanish actress Astrid Bergès-Frisbey as Syrena, a mermaid who doesn't share the lethal instincts of her fellow aquatic enchantresses. With the story arc of Will Turner and Elizabeth Swann completed, there was room for a new romantic angle. It was found in the odd but alluring pairing of the missionary and the mermaid.

In addition to such powerhouse performers as Depp, Rush, Cruz, and McShane, Bruckheimer and Marshall populated their film with an unusually strong cast of international talent (mostly British). Among the supporting players were Keith Richards (repeating his role as Captain Teague), the gifted Stephen Graham as the scruffy Scrum, Richard Griffiths as a deliciously overripe King George, Shakespearean greats Roger Allam and Anton Lesser as two of the king's men, and, in a hilarious little cameo, Dame Judi Dench as a society matron momentarily wooed by Captain Jack.

In the summer of 2010, Bruckheimer and Marshall would take their *On Stranger Tides* cast and crew to the gorgeously lush Hawaiian islands of Kauai and Oahu for two months of filming. That was followed by a few weeks of studio work back

in L.A., a few days in Puerto Rico, and finally, as a striking contrast to the verdant tropical climes, two and a half more months of filming in Great Britain. There, the filmmakers utilized myriad locations in London: the Old Royal Naval College in Greenwich, the historic Hampton Court Palace (where Henry VIII once cavorted with a few of his ill-fated wives), and Knole (a stately mansion in Kent originally built by the Archbishop of Canterbury). They also made use of seven stages at Pinewood Studios, including the massive "007 Stage" (the largest in Europe) for the elaborate sets.

On Stranger Tides opened internationally on May 20, 2011, and the film had its share of fervent admirers from the ranks of reviewers. The highly respected Ann Hornaday of *The Washington Post* wrote:

"Watching *Pirates of the Caribbean: On Stranger Tides* is to be reminded of 2003, when many skeptics (including yours truly) approached the first installment with a combination of suspicion and outright cynicism. A movie based on a theme park ride? How good could it be? Plenty good, as it turned out. And in a similar fashion, the fourth installment dispels many fans' trepidation regarding sequels and the diminishing returns they so often represent. The legions of filmgoers who have made the Pirates movies such a box office behemoth needn't worry. *On Stranger Tides* feels as fresh and bracingly exhilarating as the day Jack Sparrow first swashed his buckle, infusing new reckless energy into a franchise that shows no signs of furling its sails."

Confirming Bruckheimer's own thoughts, Hornaday also exhibited a healthy appreciation for what the new director brought to the proceedings:

"In fact, the whole of *On Stranger Tides* could be described as appropriate, clear, and neat, as first-time Pirates director Rob Marshall swiftly and without fuss delivers the action set pieces and eye-popping escapism the series has come to stand for. Starting with a smartly staged escape from King George's castle and a rollicking carriage chase through the London streets, *On Stranger Tides* delivers its whammies with metronomic regularity and, on at least two occasions, genuine ingenuity: Marshall, who started life as a choreographer in musical theater, brings those gifts strongly to bear on a stunt in which a mutinous crew is hung by their ship's lines, swinging and dangling with balletic grace. Later, a group of men watch mesmerized as an ethereal school of mermaids encircles their boat, their sinuous movements enchanting the audience just as a seductively."

Critics had their say, and audiences certainly had theirs. Around the world, there was a veritable avalanche of enthusiasm to the tune of $256.3 million from nearly 2,000 screens in more than 100 markets. This was not only the best overseas opener for the franchise, but the all-time record breaker for an international debut (edging out previous record holder *Harry Potter and the Half-Blood Prince* and up 20 percent from *At World's End*). In its first five days, *On Stranger Tides* amassed a staggering cumulative box office total of $346.4 million. Among the film's other milestones were the fourth-biggest global opening of all time, the biggest opening day and weekend of all time in the "emerging market" of Russia, and the fifth-biggest domestic opening in the long history of The Walt Disney Studios. Less than a week after opening globally, *On Stranger Tides* had already amassed more than $400 million. And against huge new summer competition, the film hung on to its first-place global position in its second and third weekends, dominating such films as *The Hangover Part II*, *Kung Fu Panda 2*, and *X-Men: First Class*.

By the fourth weekend, the international figures alone surpassed the entire box office take of *The Curse of the Black Pearl*, and it also took first position on that date as

the year's top-grossing film in North America as well—not an easy task considering the lingering economic recession. Incredibly, despite (or perhaps because of) its recovery from the devastating March 2011 tsunami and ensuing nuclear reactor crisis, Japan demonstrated its passion for the franchise (and its unfettered enthusiasm for the films of both Johnny Depp and Jerry Bruckheimer) by leading the rest of the world (except for the U.S.) in *On Stranger Tides* box office results, with the film topping that country's charts for six consecutive weeks.

On July 2, 2011, *On Stranger Tides* became only the eighth film in the history of motion pictures to cross the landmark $1 billion figure, following not far behind the final figure amassed by *Dead Man's Chest*.

Pirates of the Caribbean: On Stranger Tides was representative of a shifting paradigm in which the primacy of North American box office for big studio "tent-pole" movies was ebbing in favor of the wider international marketplace. Along with that, the film's success led to growing recognition that globalization had finally and truly swept over Hollywood—which now created films for the world and not just for the U.S. But it wasn't just about dollars, euros, yen, yuan, and rubles. The measure of the franchise's success is the fans. The numbers are a reflection of the film's huge popularity around the world, and the ability of the Pirates movies—and Jerry Bruckheimer—to break down all cultural and linguistic barriers in a kind of international Pirates party.

NATIONAL TREASURE: MAKING HISTORY COOL AGAIN

The most recent franchise launched by Jerry Bruckheimer started with *National Treasure* (2004), which can be described as a "process" movie—a movie

that immerses the audience in the action so that they become participants as opposed to mere spectators. It also happened that the film was entrenched in one of Bruckheimer's favorite subjects: the history of the United States. Bruckheimer, director Jon Turteltaub, and their screenwriters (Jim Kouf, Marianne Wibberley, Cormac Wibberley, and, uncredited, Ted Elliott and Terry Rossio) wanted to find a way to make American history come alive for family audiences in a format that was thoroughly entertaining and not the least bit didactic.

The story of *National Treasure* originated with Oren Aviv, at that time president of Buena Vista Pictures Marketing (and later the head of production for the studio), and his creative partner, Charles Segars. Their idea revolved around a man who is forced to steal the most valuable document in American history—the Declaration of Independence— when the document proves to be in dire danger, because it contains a secret treasure map. Aviv and Segars brought the project to Jon Turteltaub, a director whose professionalism and genuine light, charming touch had already been demonstrated in films such as *Cool Runnings* and *While You Were Sleeping* (both of which had been hits for Disney). All parties then engaged Jerry Bruckheimer's interest, knowing that he could shepherd the project to fruition in his inimitable style. The producer saw an opportunity to create a "four quadrant" movie that would appeal to all demographics, something truly "for the whole family."

Bruckheimer knew that the key to the story would be the various clues that lead the characters from one part of the story to another. "When you make a treasure-hunt movie," he says, "I think the clues that lead you forward have to be really smart and based on true history, which is what we did with *National Treasure*. We take simple things, like the dollar bill, which is something you use every day but never really look at, and we reveal secrets that are hidden in it. After you see this film, you'll look at the dollar in a whole new way."

When it came time for casting the film, Bruckheimer knew exactly who he wanted: Nicolas Cage. Cage was certainly the right fit for Turteltaub, who had been a classmate and friend of the actor from their days at Beverly Hills High School. "Nic epitomizes the kind of hero I respond to," says Bruckheimer. "He's leading-man handsome, yet he's also an Everyman. He's wild and weird and funny, yet he's mainstream. He's also smart, inquisitive, and passionate—just like his character, Ben Gates."

Gates is one of the most unusual, unexpected heroes of recent film history, a quirky, unpredictable intellectual, historian, and amateur cryptologist with a keen fascination for the past. "Benjamin Franklin Gates is a movie hero of the old school," astutely noted Ann Hornaday in her review of the second film, *National Treasure*: *Book of Secrets* (2007). "[He's a] dashing treasure hunter with an obsessive interest in American history. Played by Nicolas Cage in the 2004 hit *National Treasure*, Gates emerged as a new kind of leading man, one with the brains of [historian] Stephen Ambrose and the brawn of Indiana Jones. His idea of adventure is less to scale tall buildings than plumb the depths of the National Archives."

This view worked its way from the film into its marketing. That's not a high-powered rifle or bazooka slung across Ben Gates's shoulders in the print ad of *National Treasure*, but a case containing the Declaration of Independence, one of the greatest documents in all of human history. For Ben Gates and the filmmakers of *National Treasure*, the mind is more powerful than the sword.

Joining Cage, as his unlikely cohorts, were Justin Bartha, as computer expert/nerd Riley Poole; German star Diane Kruger, as archivist Abigail Chase; and Jon Voight, as Ben's equally brainy father, university professor Patrick Henry Gates (who, like his son, is named after a Revolutionary-era hero).

With the story taking the characters on a swift pursuit through Washington, D.C.; Philadelphia; and New York City, and some of the most famous sites of the American historical landscape (Independence Hall, Lincoln Memorial, Library of Congress, New York's Trinity Church), *National Treasure* really struck a chord upon its November 2004 opening. The film grossed almost exactly the same large amount of money both domestically ($173 million) and internationally ($174 million), totaling $347 million worldwide.

The film was appreciated by critics as well. Michael Sragow of *The Baltimore Sun* called the film, "A wholesome, headlong extravaganza." *The Washington Post*'s Stephen Hunter noted that, "Cleverness can be overrated, but it can be underrated too, and the best thing about *National Treasure* is how clever it is. Cage is portrayed as a nebbishy genius, not a man of force or coolness, and his solution to the problems of the [National] Archives installation is low-tech, clever, smooth, and witty."

As always, Bruckheimer was in no way confident that the first National Treasure would become the success story that it did. "I'm always surprised when an audience likes what we do," he admits. "You know, we make these movies in a kind of vacuum; we have nobody telling us what's right and wrong. It all comes from instinct and surrounding ourselves with talented people. It takes just as much hard work on a picture that doesn't work for an audience as one that does, so you're always pleasantly surprised when they're excited by a movie.

"I also love history, and learning about it myself," adds Bruckheimer. "But you know, just laying a bunch of historical facts on the screen is going to bore an audience half to death, including me. So, what we had to do to make *National Treasure* a real adventure was to find facts that audiences might not know much about, make it exciting to discover, and put the characters in jeopardy. And unfortunately for Ben, Abigail, and Riley, they got into a lot of jeopardy! When the first film opened, some people said that it was a wonderful American movie, but nobody outside of the U.S. would see it. As it turned out, our foreign box office was the same as our domestic box office, so it just goes to show that people all over the world responded to the same thing about *National Treasure*. If you make a fun movie, they will all come."

Three years later, in 2007, Bruckheimer, Turteltaub, and Cage reunited for *National Treasure*: *Book of Secrets*. After his astonishing discovery of the riches of the Knights Templar in the first film, Ben has become the world's most famous treasure hunter—although he prefers the term "treasure protector." In *Book of Secrets*, Ben and his father, university professor Patrick Gates (Jon Voight), are shaken by the discovery of one of the long-lost pages from the diary of Lincoln assassin John Wilkes Booth. The diary was found on Booth's body when he was tracked down and killed several days after murdering the president; however, several pages had been torn from the diary and had never been found . . . until now. Surprisingly, the information on one of the pages seems to implicate one of their ancestors, Thomas Gates, as a coconspirator in the assassination of President Lincoln.

With his family's name in jeopardy, Ben must work with Abigail Chase and Riley Poole in a globe-trotting adventure that crisscrosses the inner sanctums of Washington, D.C.; Paris; London; and the American heartland. Once again, Bruckheimer and the National Treasure name opened doors to nearly impossible locations for movie sets here and abroad: among them (in Washington, D.C.) Lafayette Park (which fronts the White House just across Pennsylvania Avenue), the Capitol Reflecting Pool, the Lincoln Memorial, and the Jefferson Building of the Library of Congress (again); in nearby Virginia, the grounds just outside of the main house of Mount Vernon, home to George and Martha Washington; in South Dakota, the Mount Rushmore National Memorial; in England, the exteriors of the royal Buckingham and St. James's palaces, the palatial interior of Lancaster House (which doubled for Buckingham Palace's interior), and the Old Royal Naval College in Greenwich; and in Paris, the Bir-Hakeim Bridge near the Eiffel Tower. Massive sets of underground ruins were also designed by Dominic Watkins and constructed on the Universal Studios' back lot and soundstages.

As Ben, Patrick, Abigail, and Riley meticulously unravel clues that threaten to turn history, and their lives, completely upside down, their search for historical truth widens into a hunt for perhaps the most mysterious and highly guarded book on earth, and from that, to a famed mythological treasure. Much to Patrick's consternation, Ben calls upon a secret weapon—his formidable mother and Patrick's ex-wife, linguistics professor Emily Appleton (Helen Mirren)—who hasn't spoken to Patrick in thirty-two years. She is soon caught up in the intrigue, but the team is not alone in its pursuit. The man who brought the lost page to Ben's attention, Mitch Wilkinson (Ed Harris), has his own family history to uncover. But his ambitions are less noble than merely discovering treasure, putting him on a deadly collision course with the others in a desperate effort to uncover the secrets that lie beneath the half-burnt diary page from America's past.

"What's exciting about the National Treasure movies is that you have to think to stay with it, and follow the clues," Bruckheimer noted before the movie's release. "I think that aspect really added to the success of the first film, and with the terrific cast, wonderful director, fabulous writers, and the rest of our phenomenal troops on the second, we can expect not only more of the same, but even better and bigger. Jon Turteltaub is a brilliant director who was known more for his comedies than for adventure films, so he really cut his teeth with the first film. He said, 'Whoa, this is kind of fun; maybe we should up the ante on the second one,' and he certainly did.

"What's key in making a sequel is getting the same talent behind the camera as in front of the camera," continued Bruckheimer. "We got Jon Turteltaub and the same writers back to attempt to make an even better film than the first. Then you've got to get the same actors in front of the camera, and that's key as well. We did it on the Pirates of the Caribbean movies, and we've done it again on National Treasure, on which both Nicolas Cage and Jon Voight are in sequels for the first time in their careers. Then we've added some exciting new elements, including Helen Mirren and Ed Harris. Ted Elliott and Terry Rossio, and the Wibberleys, did a brilliant job in creating this movie's characters."

National Treasure: Book of Secrets considerably outgrossed the first entry, bringing in $219 million domestically and $237 million internationally—and it even won some more love from the critics. Continuing her review in *The Washington Post*, Ann Hornaday noted that, "Cage is back in crackling good form . . . and it's clear that with this installment, the filmmakers intend for the franchise to resuscitate the derring-do and lighthearted entertainment of Saturday matinee serials of yore. And as a larky popcorn romp, *Book of Secrets* indeed recalls those classics. . . ."

Added Peter Hartlaub, of the *San Francisco Chronicle*, ". . . it's a welcome throwback to the kind of family-friendly PG moviemaking that we used to get in the early 1980s, when only the bad guys had guns, our heroes had multiple doctorates, and an eighty-year-old could enjoy the film on the same level as his ten-year-old grandson."

While nothing can ever be predicted, it seems clear enough that as long as audiences crave more entries in such already established Bruckheimer franchises as Pirates of the Caribbean, National Treasure, and Bad Boys, there's great potential for more films to come to pass. *The Lone Ranger* certainly carries a hint of that promise. But true to his word, Bruckheimer refuses to speculate on the future. "I'm too busy worrying about the present," he confesses. "The audience alone will determine what comes next.

BEVERLY HILLS COP

OPPOSITE PAGE, BOTTOM LEFT:
Director Martin Brest explains a shot to Jerry Bruckheimer
and Don Simpson on the set of Beverly Hills Cop.

BEVERLY HILLS COP II

TOP LEFT:
Director Tony Scott and Eddie Murphy on the set of
Beverly Hills Cop II.

BOTTOM LEFT:
Tony Scott consults with Don Simpson and Jerry
Bruckheimer on the Beverly Hills Cop II *set.*

BAD BOYS

TOP RIGHT:
Don Simpson, Jerry Bruckheimer, and director Michael Bay
watch the monitor during a Bad Boys camera setup.

BAD BOYS II

TOP RIGHT:
Jerry Bruckheimer indulges in his love of photography,
taking pictures on the set of Bad Boys II.

BOTTOM RIGHT:
Michael Bay ponders his next shot of Bad Boys II.

PIRATES OF THE CARIBBEAN: DEAD MAN'S CHEST

PIRATES OF THE CARIBBEAN: AT WORLD'S END

NATIONAL TREASURE

PAGE 261, TOP RIGHT:
Nicolas Cage, Jerry Bruckheimer, and
Jon Turteltaub watch monitor replay of a
scene from National Treasure: Book of Secrets.

PAGE 257, MIDDLE RIGHT:
Jerry Bruckheimer, Executive Producer and
Jerry Bruckheimer Films President of Production
Chad Oman, and director Jon Turteltaub on
the set of National Treasure.

PAGE 261, BOTTOM LEFT:
Jerry Bruckheimer on the period Washington, D.C.,
street set of National Treasure: Book of Secrets,
which was created on the back lot of Universal Studios.

NATIONAL TREASURE: BOOK OF SECRETS

CSI: CRIME SCENE INVESTIGATION

COLD CASE

THE AMAZING RACE

CSI: NY

THE EVIDENCE NEVER LIES:
LIGHTNING STRIKES TELEVISION

"We approach TV as a serious business; it's not a sideline for us. We're passionate about it; we put enormous energy into it."
—Jerry Bruckheimer to journalist Michael Schneider, *Variety*, July 10, 2006

It's hard to comprehend that in many places around the globe, TV viewers may not even be aware of Jerry Bruckheimer the movie producer. The Jerry Bruckheimer they know is the one whose ubiquitous television programs are viewed weekly by an estimated 240 million people in the United States and around the world. At the end of the 2013 broadcast season, Jerry Bruckheimer Television celebrated 1,556 episodes of television, a staggering number by any standards. And in the 2005–2006 season alone, Bruckheimer had an unprecedented ten shows airing at the same time, a feat that has never been equaled. There was one week in 2004 when, respectively, *CSI: Crime Scene Investigation*, *Without a Trace*, *CSI: Miami*, *The Amazing Race* and *Cold Case* were all top-ten, highest-rated shows. From 2003 to 2010 Jerry Bruckheimer Television was responsible for an astonishing sixteen new series.

However many shows Jerry Bruckheimer beams in the U.S. and throughout the world at any given time, his JBTV team of Jonathan Littman, Executive Vice President KristieAnne Reed, and Senior Vice President Mike Azzolino (who joined the company in 2005) are always spinning dozens of potential projects and pilots. "Television is always hit and miss," says Bruckheimer. "But we're really proud of the contributions we've made, and hope to continue to make, to the medium. We've done really well with procedurals, but also want to continue exploring the other genres as well, including comedy and reality shows. We're always examining ways of reinventing and reinvigorating television. There's still so much potential yet to be discovered."

"Jerry changed the landscape of television by making it more cinematic," confirms Jonathan Littman, president of Jerry Bruckheimer Television since 1997. "Prior to *CSI*," Littman continues, "there was not a great deal of emphasis placed on the visual signature of a television show. It was Jerry's belief that visual storytelling was equally as important as a strong narrative and strong characters. Given the number of shows since *CSI* that have emulated its style, it is clear to see the landmark change left on the television landscape."

Through the years, TV series producers, writers, and show runners allowed the lesser scope of the medium to dictate a limited vision of what was possible to achieve in television. Although there has obviously been great television through the years, an in-the-box, formulaic mode of thinking began to take hold that seemed to demand that television should look, sound, and feel like, well, television. This became a synonym for small, by the numbers, and unsurprising.

The producer's success in the TV medium is an accurate reflection of what he's accomplished in feature motion pictures, and the reason is that, as KristieAnne Reed put it, "We like to say that Jerry brought the concept of 'feature television.' The production values, cinematography, production design, and the overall visual aesthetic of television changed dramatically with *CSI*. Jerry wanted the shows to look as great as the movies did, so we set out to find the artists who could translate that feature aesthetic for the small screen. Jerry set the new bar in television, and now all networks expect your show to have a strong visual signature."

But the producer was not willing to see the backbone of story and character get steamrolled by visuals alone. Bruckheimer's philosophy of how to make a successful show was expressed with a succinct formula: "The very first thing Jerry said to me when I met with him about starting a TV division and making television more visual was, 'People watch TV with their thumbs. You have to get them to stop flipping and then hold them with a great story,'" recalls Littman. "Jerry realized early on that the audience wants, either on the big screen or the small screen, a compelling story well told. He also puts a great deal of emphasis on truly entering a unique world and learning about that world. He has never felt that TV needed to be 'small' as opposed to equally large in scope and ambition. He is probably the first producer to realize the impact of high-definition television and what that meant producing TV series."

Considering his childhood, it was as inevitable that Jerry Bruckheimer would turn to television as it was for him to produce movies; his love for both media was considerable as an only child growing up in Detroit. "Television gave me a lot, it really did," Bruckheimer told Charlie Rose on his PBS interview program in 2003. "When I grew up, I was glued to that TV. That was my entertainment. My house was always silent. My mother never had the radio on, there was nothing ever going on except me coming home and watching television. And I loved watching *Combat*, *Wanted: Dead or Alive*, and *Bonanza*; all those wonderful shows. I want to kind of give that back. I watch Dick Wolf and all these different guys who are making wonderful television, and I said, 'I can do that. I can try and do that, anyway.'"

Bruckheimer's initial foray into television was his limited involvement with the 1996–1997 ABC series version of his feature film *Dangerous Minds*, in which Annie Potts portrayed inner-city schoolteacher LouAnne Johnson. In 1997, the first fully produced series from Bruckheimer was *Soldier of Fortune, Inc.* (1997–1999), a syndicated action series about a group of highly trained covert military operatives who join forces to become an elite fighting unit. The series was certainly in line with the kind of hard-charging action films Bruckheimer

was producing at the time, and made some impact on the marketplace with its thirty-seven episodes.

Assisting Bruckheimer in that initial effort was Jonathan Littman, who the producer brought in to jump-start Jerry Bruckheimer Television in 1997 following Littman's six-year stint as a current programming and drama development executive at Fox TV. Bruckheimer and Littman began the serious work of creating a TV empire to not only match, but exceed, the likes of Aaron Spelling, Steven Bochco, John Wells, Dick Wolf, and David E. Kelley.

CSI: THE FRANCHISE

The foundation of this new television behemoth came in the form of a program entitled *CSI: Crime Scene Investigation*, which changed the shape of television as volcanically as Bruckheimer's features had altered the landscape of the feature-films arena. "It was the turn of a new century, and we thought it might be the right time for a different kind of American crime show," recalls Bruckheimer. "This genre had been done to death over the years, and was definitely ready for a reboot. On television, crimes had always been dealt with by law enforcement in the standard ways: fisticuffs, car chases, or gunplay. But Anthony Zuiker, who pitched the show to us, had other ideas. The O. J. Simpson trial had sparked interest in forensics, and Anthony's concept was of a forensic team in Las Vegas sorting through huge jigsaw puzzles and assembling the big picture through forensic science, using their brains and the most high-tech equipment possible."

What resulted was a program that is officially the most-watched television show in the world, the recipient of thirty-nine Emmy nominations, and the foundation of a franchise that has now included two spin-off shows, video games, books, comics, a museum exhibition, a

theme park attraction, and countless imitators. As the show's tagline aptly goes, "The evidence never lies."

Unbelievably, *CSI* came perilously close to never happening. "*CSI* was the last script sold to CBS that season in October, it was the last script they picked up to pilot, and it was the last pilot picked up to series," says Jonathan Littman. "Then, just before we went into production, Disney pulled out of the show and would no longer finance it. Alliance Atlantis came in and saved the day to pick up the deficit financing, and we were able to shoot."

CSI boldly and proudly announced itself during its October 6, 2000, premiere episode on CBS with the opening power chords of the Who's "Who Are You" and neon-lit images of Las Vegas, a city of secrets ready to be uncovered. Conventional heroes are not traditionally introduced by dialogue like, "Here comes the nerd squad," as one cop says to the other when Gil Grissom (William Petersen) and his team approach a crime scene in the pilot episode.

"Seeing Grissom on his knees in a suspect's toilet picking up a tiny piece of clipped toenail with a pair of tweezers is hardly a romantic image," notes Bruckheimer. "But it's a real one. *CSI* is a police procedural, but it's also a process show, which, like our movies, takes the audience deep into a world they've never been part of. We tried to make the viewer a participant, taking them inside of the investigations, the science of it all, and into the lives of the protagonists. We invite them to join the characters in the solving of each mystery, so it becomes something of an interactive experience for the viewer, luring them into each episode as amateur criminologists."

As director of the pilot episode, Danny Cannon set the dark, moody visual tone of the show in a style that's become something of a signature in other Bruckheimer series. Since then, *CSI* has attracted several feature film directors of note, including Quentin Tarantino, William Friedkin, and Martha Coolidge. The graphic nature of the program—understandable, considering the subject matter—brought television into a new level of maturity. In the middle of its first season, Les Moonves, President of CBS and someone who has worked in close associaton with Bruckheimer for many years, moved *CSI* to Thursday night, putting it in competition with NBC's dominant comedies. Amazingly, *CSI* won the time slot right away, which made the show an even more gigantic hit and changed the entire landscape of Thursday-night television. By the end of its first season, *CSI: Crime Scene Investigation* had overtaken the ratings giant *ER*, which had been the number-one show on television for years.

The cast has remained remarkably stable for a show that has been on the air for more than a decade. George Eads (Nick Stokes), Eric Szmanda (Greg Sanders), and Paul Guilfoyle (Captain Jim Brass) have been with the show from day one. But still, there have been inevitable changes. The hugely popular William Petersen was replaced as the lead in season nine by Laurence Fishburne (as Dr. Raymond Langston); Jorja Fox, who played Sara Sidle, left as a regular in season eight, but continues to appear as a special guest star; and Gary Dourdan's character, Warrick Brown, died on the first episode of season nine.

With the announcement in June 2011 that Laurence Fishburne was leaving the show before it entered its twelfth season, *CSI* was presented with yet another opportunity to refresh itself, which it accomplished with the casting in mid-July of bona fide TV star and multiple Emmy and Golden Globe Award-winner Ted Danson as D. B. Russell, the CSI team's graveyard shift supervisor. "Well, it's official," wrote Mary McNamara in the *Los Angeles Times* after Danson's initial appearance on the program. "At this stage in his career, there is nothing that Ted Danson can't do. . . .

Watching Danson glide through the first two episodes . . . is like watching Fred Astaire dance—he makes it look not only easy but inevitable." Several other critics joined McNamara in her praise of the veteran actor, and the program was suddenly born again. Also in June of 2011, it was announced that *CSI: Crime Scene Investigation* had won the International Television Audience Award for a Drama TV Series for the second consecutive year (and for the fourth time in the award's six-year history) at the Monte Carlo TV Festival, honoring it as the most watched TV drama in the world.

About six months later, Marg Helgenberger (Catherine Willows) announced her departure, although she would return for occasional guest appearances. In order to fill her substantial shoes, Elisabeth Shue, an Academy Award nominee for *Leaving Las Vegas*, would be brought in as the new female lead in the role of Julie Finlay.

The monumental success of *CSI* was not something that either Bruckheimer or Littman was willing to predict. "We knew the show was unique and that there wasn't anything like it on TV at the time," the latter notes. "But during the summer before we premiered, *The Fugitive* was the 'big show.' No one expected *CSI* to break out of the gate the way it did."

Fall 2002 saw the advent of the first CSI: Crime Scene Investigation franchise spin-off, bringing the action to southern Florida in *CSI: Miami*. Although the template was very much the same as *CSI: Crime Scene Investigation*, the show demonstrated the strength of JBTV programs in creating a team of new and compelling characters while promoting strong visual and design elements, albeit altered for the south Florida landscape. Once again, a rock anthem from the Who blasts off each show; this time it's "Won't Get Fooled Again."

The ensemble cast was headed by David Caruso as Lieutenant Horatio Caine, the role that restored him to

television superstardom, and the show saw such actors as Kim Delaney, Emily Procter, Adam Rodriguez, Rory Cochrane, Khandi Alexander, Eddie Cibrian, and Omar Benson Miller come and go throughout the series' run. In the March 1, 2010, edition of the *Los Angeles Times*, writer Jon Weinbach noted that *CSI: Miami* "has managed to carve out its own identity while staying true to the CSI formula of stylized crime, smarty-pants detective work, and, of course, a theme song by the Who. . . . Compared to the original *CSI* and *CSI: NY*, the second spin-off of the franchise that debuted in 2004, Miami has a distinct visual style that incorporates south Florida's tropical colors and sun-kissed, international vibe. Scenes are bathed in golden light, the ocean appears as an impossible shade of blue, the sky looks blood-orange, and there are bright pastels all over the show."

Premiering on September 22, 2004, *CSI: NY* was the second CBS show to spin off from the blockbuster JBTV CSI franchise. The Manhattan forensics team is led by a hardened former marine, Mac Taylor (Gary Sinise), who is imbued with a strong mandate to protect the city and his country. Like its sister CSI shows, a Who song ("Baba O'Riley") is used as the opening theme for *CSI: NY*. Over the years, the show became a hip destination for a list of major names from the worlds of film, music, and sports making guest-star appearances. Unlike its sister shows, set in glamorous Las Vegas and Miami, *CSI: NY* took the franchise to a less glitzy, grittier city, and immediately joined the other two as a formidable network television presence.

All three shows combined for a historic "CSI Crossover Trilogy," a three-part story that aired in November 2009. And crossovers synergistically link JBTV shows together from time to time, indicating that all operate in the same universe. For a show that almost didn't make it onto the air, *CSI* and its offspring now boast an impressive distribution:

they air in more than 160 countries, with reruns in wide syndication and spread out over numerous cable stations. It is, in short, an international phenomenon of the medium, and has wielded a mighty influence on subsequent programs which didn't hesitate to borrow its style and, often, content as well. The show's popularity remains undimmed and has also boosted a huge public interest in forensics and science, as evidenced by the traveling interactive exhibition "CSI: The Experience," developed for the Science Museum Exhibit Collaborative by the Fort Worth Museum of Science and History in partnership with CBS and the National Science Foundation. The exhibit debuted at Chicago's heralded Museum of Science and Industry in May 2007 and has toured museums and science centers all over the United States, Europe, and Asia. The world truly became CSI's laboratory.

JBTV TAKES OFF

At the outset of 2001, Jerry Bruckheimer Television began an unrivaled run, placing more shows on network schedules than any other company ever had, while maintaining four massive franchise shows. And on average, JBTV has put two shows on the Fall schedule every year but two since then, comprising an astonishing seventeen shows in seven years.

Premiering in September 2001—one week before 9/11—was another phenomenon from Jerry Bruckheimer Television, a reality competition show that quite literally conquered the world: *The Amazing Race*. Created by Bertram Van Munster and Elise Doganieri, and hosted by New Zealand-born Phil Keoghan, *The Amazing Race* entered the field of reality shows ahead of the onslaught of unscripted programming, when only *Survivor* was on the air. Rather than positioning the contestants in one geographic location, the show made a playing field of the entire globe, thus turning each episode into not only a suspenseful competition, but a hugely

entertaining travelogue as well. ". . . The closest a reality show has ever got to being a critical darling" is how Joel Stein described the program in a May 2003 *Time* magazine profile of Bruckheimer. *The Amazing Race* was proof positive that reality shows could succeed on positive vibes and a joyful, uplifting celebration of the planet we inhabit.

Each season has featured several teams comprised of two people who were connected either by marriage, romance, family relationship, or friendship. These teams race around the world, engage in a huge array of tasks in each country (mostly physical), and attempt to arrive first at "pit stops" at the end of each leg. The last team to arrive is subject either to elimination or disadvantages on the next leg. The ultimate prize for coming in first in the final leg is a cool one million dollars. Along the way relationships and alliances are forged, tested, destroyed, or forever altered. What characterizes each season is the joy of traveling and experiencing other cultures, while participants use brain and body to overcome every obstacle. The viewer, meanwhile, enjoys not only the armchair travel, but also getting to know the contestants from week to week and cheering for their favorites.

The Amazing Race has now won an astonishing nine prime-time Emmy Awards in the category of Reality Program—Competition, seven of which were taken consecutively.

In August 2011, almost a decade after the debut of *The Amazing Race*, Bruckheimer reunited with *The Amazing Race* producers Bertram Van Munster and Elise Doganieri for a genre-bending and highly original six-episode competition show, *Take the Money & Run*, which pits real-life cops against everyday people trying to conceal the location of a $100,000 cash prize.

Profiles from the Front Line (2003) was another reality show from Jerry Bruckheimer Television, but this is where the similarities ended. The show was vastly different from

The Amazing Race, and ultimately much more controversial. The ABC series offered the viewer up-close-and-personal chronicles of members of the U.S. Special Operations Forces who had been dispatched to Afghanistan following the 9/11 tragedy, and those preparing for action preceding the U.S. invasion of Iraq. In the All Movie Guide Web site, Hal Erickson wrote, "The program succeeded in putting a human face on war not by luridly stressing its dangers and horrors or by adhering to an artificial, prepared script, but through the poignant words and thoughts of the soldiers themselves."

Profiles from the Front Line once again paired Bruckheimer with Bertram Van Munster, and could in a sense be seen as a reality-television companion to *Black Hawk Down*, which had been released less than two years before and featured dramatized and deeply respectful depictions of several Special Forces soldiers during the 1993 Battle of Mogadishu. In a 2003 interview with Charlie Rose, Bruckheimer commented, "You look at the young men and young women who sacrificed their families, sacrificed a big part of their lives and [are] not getting paid a lot of money to go overseas and work in horrendous situations that are very dangerous. You see kids getting killed every day in Iraq, which is a terrible situation. They give it all up, because they believe in this country. I believe we should know about them. I believe we should know what they do every day and how committed they are to what they do," he stated. "They are what make this country great. We're not Hollywood-izing. We're just telling you what they do. We might add a little music to it and make it look a little sexier than what they actually do, but their lives are portrayed on television the way it really is."

CRIME AND LEGAL PROCEDURALS . . . WITH A DIFFERENCE

One of Jerry Bruckheimer Television's greatest

accomplishments was to take the "procedural" format to an entirely new level, first with the CSI programs and then with a number of similarly provocative programs.

Jerry Bruckheimer Television followed *CSI: Crime Scene Investigation* and *CSI: Miami* with another big success that premiered on September 26, 2002, and ran for seven seasons. Created by Hank Steinberg, *Without a Trace* was, according to Jonathan Littman, "born of America's fascination with the Chandra Levy murder case, with its creative roots in *Laura*, one of the great noir films of the 1940s." Despite its vintage inspiration, *Without a Trace* was also a highly contemporary procedural that traced, with similar detail and accuracy as *CSI*, the cases of an FBI unit specializing in missing-persons investigations. The show was certainly another "process" program, taking viewers inside the investigation and the private, and often secret, lives of the victims through stylish flashbacks and haunting ghost images. Equally as intriguing were the complex lives of the agents themselves, played by a strong cast headed by Anthony LaPaglia and Poppy Montgomery. *Without a Trace* was notable for the inclusion, at the end of most episodes, of information about real-life missing persons. "We wanted to emphasize that although our stories were fiction, they were based on real and very tragic disappearances," Bruckheimer notes. "It was really important to us to call attention to the reality and gravity of these situations."

Without a Trace went up against perennial favorite *ER*, and overtook it in the number of households viewing the programs. It was also the first Golden Globe Award winner for a Jerry Bruckheimer Television program, with Anthony LaPaglia taking home the prize for his portrayal of Jack Malone.

Cold Case (created by Meredith Stiehm), which premiered on September 28, 2003, was Bruckheimer's next procedural hit for CBS and Warner Bros. Television. Its pilot episode, directed by Mark Pellington, introduced the signature "minimovie" flashback opening that came to epitomize the powerful JBTV aesthetic. The show chronicled the investigative work of a homicide division of the Philadelphia Police Department that specializes in cold cases—crimes that had never been solved. "We loved the idea that just because the trail may have gone cold on a crime, it doesn't mean that there's no chance for justice," says Bruckheimer. "A crime committed fifty years ago is just as terrible . . . there's no expiration date."

Alongside the plot of each individual case, strong characters were developed, particularly the lead, Detective Lilly Rush (Kathryn Morris), who suffered as the result of a dysfunctional upbringing by an alcoholic mother. The show revolutionized the use of popular music in television, with episodes built around the catalogs of such top artists and groups as Bruce Springsteen and Nirvana (both very sparing in licensing their work to films and TV). The use of period-correct music was intended to put the viewer into an instant time machine, and by the time the show had finished its highly successful seven-year run, *Cold Case* had indelibly impacted the medium with its style and intelligence.

"*Without a Trace* and *Cold Case* were two seminal television shows that took premises that nobody could ever make work on TV, and made them work through inventive storytelling and emotion," observes Jonathan Littman. "We expanded to much more emotional story lines that went to the personal side of crime, rather than the science."

Just Legal was another collaboration between Bruckheimer and Warner Bros. TV for The WB, and although the show had a brief life after its September 19, 2005, debut, it was well appreciated by critics and viewers. At the core of the show was the relationship between Grant Cooper (Don Johnson), a cynical, booze-soaked L.A. defense attorney, and nineteen-year-old David "Skip" Ross (Jay Baruchel), an idealistic legal prodigy who can't find a job because of his youth and is reluctantly taken on by Cooper.

Another legal drama, *Close to Home*, had somewhat better fortune on CBS after premiering on October 4, 2005. Jennifer Finnigan starred as deputy prosecutor Annabeth Chase, who works on cases that reveal the often-violent underbelly of her Indiana county.

Bruckheimer returned to the legal procedural format with *Justice*, a study of how the media age affects the way high-profile cases are tried. It premiered on August 30, 2006, on Fox. The cast was headed by Victor Garber, as Ron Trott, a very modern incarnation of the "gleefully amoral" lawyer who relishes the spotlight.

Eleventh Hour, an adaptation of the British series of the same title, premiered on October 9, 2008, on CBS. Created by Stephen Gallagher, it was another offbeat procedural linking crime to science and technology. The show starred Rufus Sewell as Dr. Jacob Hood, a special science adviser for the FBI, who investigates crimes that elude more conventional agents.

The aptly titled *Dark Blue* was Jerry Bruckheimer Television's initial entry into cable, premiering on TNT on July 15, 2009, and it took full advantage of the additional freedoms available outside of the more restricted network system. The show was created by Danny Cannon and Doug Jung, and merged Cannon's strong aesthetics with the Bruckheimer model, turning the show into a police procedural that takes

OPPOSITE PAGE, BOTTOM RIGHT:
Jerry Bruckheimer with his The Amazing Race *executives Elise Doganieri,*
Bertram Van Munster, and Jonathan Littman. Littman is also president
of Jerry Bruckheimer Television.

THE AMAZING RACE

WITHOUT A TRACE

COLD CASE

CLOSE TO HOME

its characters to the edge. *Dark Blue* chronicled a deep undercover unit in the Los Angeles Police Department headed by tough cop Carter Shaw (Dylan McDermott), whose obsession with his work had cost him his marriage. Additional complications stemmed from the troubles of each of his team members. These characters seemed to exist in a physical and ethical shadow world, accentuated by the show's powerful visual style and a level of graphic violence that is only possible on cable.

Bruckheimer's second 2009 show, premiering on September 22 on ABC, was similarly dark in tone and content. *The Forgotten* brought the viewer into the world of a group of amateur detectives comprising The Forgotten Network, who strive to give names and identities to John and Jane Does, numberless and faceless victims of past crimes. Their efforts almost take on a spiritual dimension, lending the series an air of melancholy—an emotion rare in network television. The Forgotten Network is comprised of haunted souls, most prominently Alex Donovan (Christian Slater), a former police officer whose eight-year-old daughter vanished. *The Forgotten* succeeded in bringing shelved cases to light, carrying on the tradition of *Without a Trace* and *Cold Case* in illuminating the darkest corners of humanity by shining a light on the victims.

The fall 2010 season saw network pickups of two JBTV pilots: the crime procedural *Chase* for NBC, and a legal drama, *The Whole Truth*, for ABC. Both programs continued the provocative and challenging tenor of Bruckheimer's television output. Starring Kelli Giddish and Cole Hauser, *Chase* was a propulsive thriller (or, as Jonathan Littman described it, "a Western with a female sheriff") about a high-priority Fugitive Task Force team based in Houston, Texas, tracking most-wanted criminals. *The Whole Truth* presented an interesting twist on legal procedurals by allowing the viewer to experience each case through the eyes of both the prosecution and defense teams, and starred Maura Tierney and Rob Morrow as friendly enemies on opposing sides.

PUSHING THE ENVELOPE

Although Jerry Bruckheimer Television is usually associated with crime and legal procedurals, just as in his features, the producer has often pushed the boundaries of his comfort zones and experimented in other genres. Taking a break from the procedural format, JBTV's other 2003 debut, in addition to *Profiles from the Front Line*, was *Skin*, for the Fox network. The provocative plot was a very twenty-first-century Romeo-and-Juliet story in which two teens fall for each other despite the feud between their fathers, a pornographer and a district attorney. The strong cast top-lined the late Ron Silver as adult entertainment kingpin Larry Goldman and Kevin Anderson as District Attorney Tom Roam, backed by Rachel Ticotin and newcomer Olivia Wilde (in her first major role).

E-Ring, which premiered on NBC on September 21 of the same year, and was created by Ken Robinson and David McKenna, was a classic Bruckheimer "process" show that brought viewers into the inner sanctum of the Pentagon, one of the most secretive establishments in the United States.

Modern Men was the first foray into situation comedy for Jerry Bruckheimer Television, but it hit a stumbling block when the show was canceled just after its March 17, 2006, debut due to a lack of time slots availability from the merger of The WB and UPN that resulted in the formation of one new network, The CW. Essentially, it was a case of the network being canceled before the show was. The series starred Eric Lively, Josh Braaten, and Max Greenfield as three lifelong friends whose love lives are in such disarray that they hire a "life coach," portrayed by Jane Seymour.

Miami Medical was Bruckheimer Television's first show set against the time-honored backdrop of a hospital. Bruckheimer's stamp brought to the genre his signature sharp visuals and characters, who not only live on the edge, but sometimes tip over onto the other side, as indicated in the program's theme song, the Rolling Stones' "19th Nervous Breakdown." Created by Jeffrey Lieber, *Miami Medical* premiered on CBS on April 2, 2010.

Bruckheimer and his JBTV team all know that television is perhaps even more challenging than feature films. "The odds, in sheer percentages, are always against you," notes the producer candidly. "Television is a tough game with a high attrition rate. You do your best, and then it's up to the audience. But you have to take the risks, do the best you can to find the best material, actors, and creative team, and hope that the viewing audience likes what they see."

Jonathan Littman points out that, "We are all over the world. Success or failure, the Bruckheimer name storms the globe, and there isn't a country where you won't turn on the TV and see a JBTV show." In addition to the numerous worldwide adaptations of *The Amazing Race*, there are now international versions of other shows as well, including localized versions of *Without a Trace* and *Cold Case* in Russia, and *Trace* being done in France as well.

"We're always excited to see how we can raise the bar a little higher in the medium," says Bruckheimer, "and we'll always keep trying to do just that." Proving that point, a new JBTV series, *Hostages*, premiered on CBS in September 2013. The provocative and suspenseful drama stars Toni Collette as a brilliant surgeon whose family is taken hostage by a rogue FBI agent, portrayed by Dylan McDermott. Also premiering in 2013 would be an unscripted drama with the tentative title *Marshal Law: Texas*, which centers on Texas Marshals who pursue the most dangerous fugitives.

CLIMB A HIGHER HILL: THE LONE RANGER AND INTO THE FUTURE

And so, almost poetically, the story has come full circle. Forty years after the release of *The Culpepper Cattle Co.*, a Western, Jerry Bruckheimer started production on a typically innovative, iconoclastic, but respectful, new version of one of the most renowned Westerns of all time, *The Lone Ranger*. Reuniting director Gore Verbinski and Johnny Depp, who first collaborated on the initial three groundbreaking Pirates of the Caribbean movies and then on the singularly and brilliantly offbeat animated film *Rango*, *The Lone Ranger* paired the superstar, portraying a Tonto unlike any seen before, with charismatic up-and-comer, Armie Hammer, as the titular defender of justice in the Old West. Set during the building of the transcontinental railroad in 1869, *The Lone Ranger* lived up to its subject matter with some of the most ambitious and complex train sequences in film history, while also keeping the focus squarely on the human comedy and drama revolving around its two "odd couple" leading characters.

In Verbinski and Bruckheimer's *The Lone Ranger*, the West is under siege by government-sanctioned, rapacious, railroad-building robber barons, not unlike Lord Cutler Beckett and his East India Trading Company of *Pirates of the Caribbean*: *Dead Man's Chest* and *Pirates of the Caribbean*: *At World's End*. And like the pirates in those films, both the Lone Ranger (aka John Reid, in this version a pragmatic law school graduate who strictly adheres to societal conventions and is fond of quoting seventeenth-century British philosopher John Locke) and the Comanche-born Tonto—because of peculiar circumstances which jettison them from their own people and cultures—become "a

band apart," in the script's sly reference to *Bande a Part* (*Band of Outsiders*), Jean-Luc Godard's 1964 classic of rebellious French cinema. "There comes a time when a good man must wear a mask. . . ." the old Tonto tells a young boy as he recounts the story of his adventures with the Lone Ranger, indicating that in order to fight evil, one must sometimes live outside of social norms.

As with *Pearl Harbor* and *Pirates of the Caribbean*: *The Curse of the Black Pearl* before it, Jerry Bruckheimer struggled to get the film in front of the cameras after a temporary shutdown. *The Lone Ranger* was developed for several years before finally targeting an October 2011 start date. It was not to be. The all-too-well chronicled shutdown occurred on August 12, 2011, with Bruckheimer and Disney then working diligently to resolve budget concerns for the next two months. Once again, the producer diplomatically and calmly steered *The Lone Ranger* back into production, with principal photography finally beginning in Albuquerque, New Mexico, on February 23, 2012.

It was a remarkable testament to the project's appeal that almost all of the fine and much-in-demand cast—Depp, Hammer, the great Golden Globe- and Emmy Award-winning veteran Tom Wilkinson, two-time Oscar and six-time Golden Globe Award nominee Helena Bonham Carter, heralded British actress Ruth Wilson of television's *Jane Eyre* and *Luther*, and the versatile, Emmy Award-winning Barry Pepper—held fast to their commitments to *The Lone Ranger*. Joining the company just before the cameras began rolling was William Fichtner, a veteran of such Jerry Bruckheimer

productions as *Armageddon* and *Black Hawk Down*.

The script was written by Bruckheimer stalwarts and Pirates veterans Ted Elliott and Terry Rossio, Eric Aronson, and Justin Haythe (*Revolutionary Road*), who was on the set nearly every day throughout production. A smart and daring reinvention, the screenplay was described by the producer as "a buddy-dramedy" version of the classic tale, which originated in January 1933 as a radio program, and later made its way to the big and small screens, first as a Republic Pictures serial and then as one of the most popular and iconic television programs of all time. Many of the highlights of the radio and television shows are present in the new version: the Lone Ranger's white stallion, Silver; the silver bullet; the villainous Butch Cavendish; and the mask created from the clothing of Reid's murdered brother, Dan. However, these memorable plot points are all cleverly refreshed and renewed, not only for a new generation that may have scant knowledge of the Lone Ranger, but for the older one that grew up with the classic tale.

"Our *Lone Ranger* is really more of an odd-couple story," explains Bruckheimer, "with two characters who are really at odds at the beginning of the film. Then, through the course of their relationship, there's a kind of uneasy bonding, because they're totally different individuals. Our Lone Ranger in the movie is a character who grew up in the West, but then decided to go east to attend law school. He's returning to his town of Colby, Texas, after graduation to be a prosecutor, believing in the strength of the law, and going by the book. Of course, Tonto comes from a very different world view. He knows the way of the West, and

knows that you sometimes have to take law and order in your own hands. It's the clash of ideas and personalities between these two characters that makes the movie so interesting. The key to the whole story that we're telling is the fact that these two men don't realize that they need each other, but they do."

Depp's interpretation of Tonto is vastly different from past portrayals of the character. Although invested with dignity by Jay Silverheels in the 1950s television series, Tonto never emerged from the "faithful Indian companion" archetype. "Johnny creates these amazing characters, no matter what movie he's in," notes Bruckheimer. "His Tonto is different from any Tonto you've seen before, a different look, a different feel, both very entertaining and moving at the same time. The story is actually told from Tonto's point of view, which in itself places him at the center of the story rather than the periphery."

Depp, who is partially of Cherokee heritage and more importantly has always harbored a deep kinship with Native Americans and other indigenous cultures, felt that he could effectively reconceive the role of Tonto and try to right what had always been an unbalanced relationship between the Lone Ranger and Tonto. "I always felt Native Americans were badly portrayed in Hollywood films over the decades," he told *Entertainment Weekly*'s Clark Collis in January 2011. "It's a real opportunity for me to give a salute to them. Tonto was a sidekick in all the Lone Ranger series. [This film] is a very different approach to that partnership. And a funny one I think."

Depp also told *The Hollywood Reporter* that ". . . I like the idea of having the opportunity to make fun of the idea of the Indian as a sidekick . . . I don't see Tonto that way."

Jerry Bruckheimer, Gore Verbinski, and Johnny Depp were all on the same page as far as the approach to the

material was concerned. "The only version of *The Lone Ranger* I'm interested in doing is *Don Quixote* told from Sancho Panza's point of view," Verbinski told the *Los Angeles Times*' Geoff Boucher in February 2011. "And hence I was honest early on with Johnny that Tonto is the part. We're not going to do it [straight]; everyone knows that story. I don't want to tell that story . . . I want the version from the untrustworthy narrator who might be a little crazy—but somehow the question is, is he crazy or is the world crazy? That, I find fascinating."

For a challenging seven months, Bruckheimer and Verbinski took their cast and crew on a filmmaking journey. The company began production on soundstages and sets (including two Western towns built from the ground up) in and around Albuquerque, and then began a road trip, which saw the production filming in some of the most iconic landscapes of the American Southwest. These sites included Monument Valley; Canyon de Chelly in Arizona and Shiprock in New Mexico (all within the boundaries of the Navajo Nation); the spectacular rock formations in Moab, Utah; and a silver mine constructed specifically for the film in the small burgh of Creede, Colorado. The physically demanding production saw the company working in temperatures ranging from twenty-five degrees Fahrenheit in the New Mexican winter and the Colorado mountain nights, to the one-hundred-degrees-plus days endured in the Moab summer.

The Lone Ranger is proof positive that after forty years of feature-film producing, not only has Jerry Bruckheimer retained every iota of energy and ambitiousness, but that his tastes are more adventurous and edgy than ever before. By championing Gore Verbinski, a visionary filmmaker who manages to combine a completely independent, even subversive sensibility with an ability to thrill mass audiences,

Bruckheimer is advancing commercial cinema into a new era.

As *The Lone Ranger* surged forth, Jerry Bruckheimer's slate remained as busy as ever. On June 3, 2013, principal photography began—primarily on locations in Bronx, New York—on *Beware the Night*, a paranormal thriller for Screen Gems that represented another change of pace for the producer. The film, directed by Scott Derrickson (*Sinister*, *The Exorcism of Emily Rose*), reunited Bruckheimer with star Eric Bana (a dozen years after helping to launch him to fame in *Black Hawk Down*), with Edgar Martinez, Joel McHale, and Olivia Munn also in the cast. Plans were already being made for the fifth entry in the Pirates of the Caribbean series, with Johnny Depp set to repeat his iconic role of Captain Jack Sparrow, under the direction of Norwegian filmmakers Joachim Ronning and Espen Sandberg (*Kon Tiki*). And on June 22, 2013, Jerry Bruckheimer achieved yet another landmark by receiving his star on the Hollywood Walk of Fame, with Disney Chairman Bob Iger and Depp himself giving introductory speeches in praise of the producer. For as long as Bruckheimer continues to do what he loves most, resting on laurels has always been positively verboten. "I'm always too worried about the next one," he confesses.

Recently, a Jerry Bruckheimer Films staffer, while discussing a project with the producer, submitted the thought that, "We're a bit ahead of the game with this one," to which he quickly responded with his characteristic smile. "We're never ahead of the game!" With forty years of accomplishments behind him, and new paths to blaze in front of him, Jerry Bruckheimer looks to the future. He always feels the wind at his back, pushing him ever forward. "I never look back," he says, echoing what he's already said many times before. "There's always another hill to climb." A hill, perhaps, that's about to be struck by lightning.

TOP LEFT:
Holding his Hollywood Walk of Fame plaque, Jerry Bruckheimer
is surrounded by friends and colleagues (left to right) Jon Voight,
director Gore Verbinski, Martin Lawrence, Johnny Depp, Tom Cruise,
and Disney Chairman and CEO Bob Iger.

BOTTOM LEFT:
Jerry Bruckheimer receives his Walk of Fame plaque from
the Hollywood Chamber of Commerce's Leron Gubler.

RIGHT:
Jerry Bruckheimer is flanked by two actors he helped
propel to the heights of fame, Johnny Depp and Tom Cruise.

PAGES 288–291: *Stephen Berkman photographed these remarkable tintypes of the leading players of* The Lone Ranger (*Johnny Depp, Armie Hammer with Jerry Bruckheimer as well as solo, William Fichtner, Helena Bonham Carter, Ruth Wilson and Bryant Prince, Tom Wilkinson*). *Using a nineteenth-century view camera and Dallmeyer lens, and utilizing the wet-collodian process, Berkman shot all of these in 100-degree-plus temperatures and post-dust storm conditions in Moab, Utah (save for the image of Bonham Carter, which was photographed on the film's Colby town set in New Mexico). The original tintypes appear as they would in a mirror—reversals of what the naked eye would see—due to the nature of the camera.*

A CONVERSATION WITH LINDA BRUCKHEIMER
"HE'S THE PEOPLE'S MOVIE PRODUCER"

Q. WHAT CHARACTERISTICS DO YOU THINK MAKE JERRY THE ENORMOUS SUCCESS THAT HE IS?

A. Jerry has a unique assortment of talents, to say the least. It is quite rare to be creative and business minded, in equal measure. With that combination on your side, you've got the situation covered. Something that often gets overlooked: he was a psychology major and that's got to figure in there somewhere.

And then there's his fantastic instinct for picking talent. Consider all the actors and directors and writers that he's worked with, many of whom he used at the very beginning of their careers: Tom Cruise, Tony Scott, Michael Bay, Michael Mann, Nicole Kidman, Will Smith . . . just to name a very few. He also takes risks—Nicolas Cage as an action star and Johnny Depp as a pirate. Those were not obvious choices at the time.

Not to lay it on too thick, but he is the most determined, persistent person you'll ever encounter. In Hollywood, where projects are often derailed by unpredictable behavior, Jerry is someone you can rely on, a logical person who means what he says. He doesn't make a lot of promises he can't keep. And he manages it all with a minimum of fanfare.

So, the bottom line is, if you ever want to get something done, give it to Jerry Bruckheimer.

Q. THERE ARE SO MANY PEOPLE WHO TALK ABOUT HIS STEALTH METHODS . . . .

A. Well, he certainly isn't a chit-chatter or a blabbermouth! He makes a plan, then zooms in under the radar, without any proclamations or braggadocio.

It's fascinating to watch him in a meeting. He can sit for an hour hardly saying a word, just listening to the ideas flying back and forth. When everyone's had their say, he'll offer his own point of view, which is generally succinct, dead right, and evidence that he absorbed every detail. And, it's usually the solution they've been seeking. People who haven't worked with him are often shocked by such precision. It is disarming and quite impressive.

Q. THAT'S A COMPLETELY RARE COMMODITY IN ANY BUSINESS, BUT ESPECIALLY IN SHOW BUSINESS.

A. A pretty unbeatable package actually, particularly in an industry that relies so heavily on razzle-dazzle. But, anybody who has been to one of Jerry's movie premieres knows he can certainly rise to the occasion . . . and then some.

Q. *I WAS WONDERING HOW JERRY CHANGED THROUGH THE YEARS, IF AT ALL. THERE SEEMS TO BE A LEVEL OF STABILITY THAT HAS ALWAYS EXISTED.*

A. Success can do peculiar things to people. But it can enhance their best qualities. As a husband, father, a friend, he's just the same old Jerry, and that's what's so refreshing. He is kind and supportive and someone I can always count on. He never steers me wrong. His core beliefs have definitely kept him on track.

As a filmmaker, success has enabled him to branch out with a variety of projects. Going from films to television, for example, gave him a tremendous amount of satisfaction. But that transition wasn't a sure thing, even though he made it look easy.

Through it all, he hasn't taken any of his success for granted. Nor does he rest on his laurels. He is as nervous about his latest project as he was his first, fretting over every detail. Even when he's on the treadmill, there are stacks of scripts and notes and DVDs. He's always reading, listening and watching. It is constant . . . and very annoying some times!

His late partner, Don Simpson, loved to tell a story that illustrated Jerry's legendary attention to detail. After watching a rough cut of one of their movies, everyone gave it a thumbs-up, except Jerry. He had two pages of notes, some of them regarding issues as seemingly insignificant as a squeaky door on reel three.

Q. *FROM WHAT I'VE READ, EVEN DURING THE HEYDAY OF THE DON SIMPSON/JERRY BRUCKHEIMER YEARS, JERRY WAS ALWAYS THE QUIET, UNPREPOSSESSING MEMBER OF THE PARTNERSHIP. HE SEEMED TO BE VERY MUCH THE SAME PERSON.*

A. Yes, Don was quite loquacious and highly dramatic and Jerry was more subdued. But don't be deceived by the absence of clatter!

Someone who worked with them during that time called Jerry "The Velvet Dagger." Sounds a bit sinister . . . but when push comes to shove, he's about the toughest customer you'll ever encounter. Nobody survives in this business for very long if they're a pushover. Jerry just doesn't flex his muscles unnecessarily, but he's the one who gets the tough jobs done.

Nobody figured this out faster than Don himself. For someone as intimidating as Don could be, surprisingly, he was very self-effacing about his own vulnerabilities and was fond of saying: "Jerry Bruckheimer is the toughest motherf----- on the planet."

More than once Don would rant and rave for days about a director or employee who was messing up, then when the decision was made to replace them, he'd turn on a dime and say, "So, uh, Jerry, could YOU fire him?"

I might add that the two of them together was a unique – and near perfect—composite. It was also a mutual admiration society.

Q. *SOMEONE TOLD ME THAT WHEN YOU'RE JERRY BRUCKHEIMER YOU DON'T NEED TO SPEAK LOUDLY. IT'S REALLY NICE THAT SOMEBODY WHO HAS THAT KIND OF POWER UNDERSTANDS THE USES OF IT RATHER THAN*

ABUSES IT.

A. Precisely. It was Benjamin Franklin who said, "Well done is better than well said." That seems to be Jerry's unofficial motto.

Q. *HE MIGHT BE THE ONLY ONE IN TOWN WHO ACTUALLY HAS THAT QUALITY.*

A. I don't know if Jerry's the only one, but it has certainly served him well. And, it's not a ploy. He is just naturally not a big talker. He's also very shy.

When he was growing up, his mother said she was always getting called to his elementary school. When she asked the teacher what was the problem, she complained that Jerry was disrupting the classroom by cracking jokes and talking too much! So, his personality has taken a slight detour.

Q. *HE TRULY NEVER TAKES A VACATION, DOES HE? EVEN WHEN HE'S ON VACATION, HE'S STILL ATTENDING TO BUSINESS?*

A. The word "vacation" might appear on a calendar, but that's sort of false advertising. In that regard, Jerry and I are lucky to have found one another since neither one us can really rest until we have our work out of the way. We do have a lot of fun together, but don't always relax in the proverbial sense of lounge chairs and sandy beaches.

When we visit our farm in rural Kentucky, we begin with a nice long walk in mind, but thirty seconds later we're making a list of trees to plant and barns to paint. And what I don't see, he does. So, it's endless. If there was a Nobel Prize for list making, we'd win it.

But that's the reality of owning property. It's a big responsibility, but we are not afraid of getting our hands dirty, literally and figuratively. We both grew up in

Linda and Jerry Bruckheimer at an industry event.

*Linda and Jerry Bruckheimer on the slopes during
one of their very brief (and usually working) holidays.*

Linda and Jerry Bruckheimer on the red carpet.

extremely modest circumstances and know what it takes to get the job done.

Q. HE SAYS THAT HE DOESN'T SEE IT AS WORK, THAT IT'S WHAT HE LOVES TO DO.
A. That's the beauty of a workaholic. We've got very creative ways to disguise actual work! The person who coined the phrase "labor of love" did an excellent job of spinning it.

Q. SO, THESE EXTRAORDINARY, WONDERFUL PROPERTIES THAT YOU HAVE, THEY'RE NOT REALLY RETREATS? MAYBE DIVERSIONS, BUT IT'S NOT LIKE YOU'RE HIDING OUT FROM THE WORLD OR FROM THE BUSINESS AT HAND.
A. Obviously, these are great complaints to have, because we're lucky to have realized so many of our dreams. Besides, this "work" to which you refer is not all drudgery. In fact, we thrive on it. The historical preservation projects in Kentucky are particularly rewarding. There is nothing more satisfying than seeing a barren field begin to yield crops, or a dilapidated building blossom back to life. We get immeasurable pride from them and they benefit the entire community. If there's DNA for caretakers, I'm sure it matches ours.

Q. YOU'VE ALREADY PARTIALLY EXPLAINED YOUR SUCCESS AS A COUPLE. THIRTY-EIGHT YEARS IS MIRACULOUS, ESPECIALLY IN HOLLYWOOD. CAN YOU EXPAND ON THAT? WHAT'S KEPT THE TWO OF YOU SO BONDED FOR SUCH A LONG TIME NOW?
A. This might sound corny or hokey, but to borrow the line from *Prince of Persia*, "Some things are destined to

be." Our relationship is one of those things. It was love at first sight, and the depth of that, connection hasn't diminished in thirty-eight years.

Because of that, I am always puzzled by people who complain that marriage is hard work. If you feel like you're on a chain gang or digging ditches, you are with the wrong person. Period. The point and the beauty of a relationship is to develop a comfort level with your partner and a barrier against the rest of the world. Marriage should be a sanctuary, not a prison.

That doesn't mean that it's free of responsibility. Jerry and I both know what's important to one another, and somehow the territory in between has never been breached. This could be tricky, becausetemperamentally, we are both so different. Fundamentally, though, we are so similar. Jerry's much calmer and I'm more expressive, maybe even . . . hotheaded. I do like to generate a lot of racket. He's very good at tuning that out, by the way!

Q. EXPRESSIVE?
A. Expressive covers a lot of bases. I mean, two hotheads don't work together, do they? In terms of logistical perfection, our personality traits really click right into place. So, that's a whole lot of luck and a whole lot of magic.

Q. CAN YOU EVER IMAGINE JERRY RETIRING OR EVER SLOWING DOWN?
A. Not really . . . especially when you consider retirement in the traditional sense of the word—that treasure that awaits at the end of a long, laborious journey. The luckiest person in the world is the one who loves their work, and work is Jerry's first love.

Q. I WANT TO KNOW WHAT YOU FEEL THE LEGACY OF HIS CAREER WILL BE. IN 150, 200, 300 YEARS, WHEN PEOPLE LOOK BACK AT THE HISTORY OF FILM AND TV, WHAT DO YOU THINK HIS PRIMARY LEGACY WILL HAVE BEEN?
A. Jerry makes films and television for one reason only— to entertain and please the crowds. And his instinct is usually pitch-perfect. Part of this comes from staying in touch with everyday people.

The driving force has always been the same: He simply loves movies. They were a tremendous influence in his life as a young boy in Detroit and the magic of those days is still the engine that keeps his vision running.

I can't help but make the full circle connection between those early days and his current ritual of going from theater to theater on the opening night of one of his films. He is very much the young boy as he stands in the back of a neighborhood movie house and monitors the crowd. Usually, there is a palpable excitement in the air when the movie is just about to start. When the curtains open and the crowd reacts to that lightning bolt on the screen, you can feel his pride of ownership.

We usually go with the intention of staying for ten or fifteen minutes, but we always stay for the entire movie, just experiencing every emotion with the crowd. He wants to see what makes them laugh or cry or applaud. For him, the applause at the end is the biggest thrill of all. It is his childhood dream in action.

So, I guess you could say that Jerry is the people's film producer.

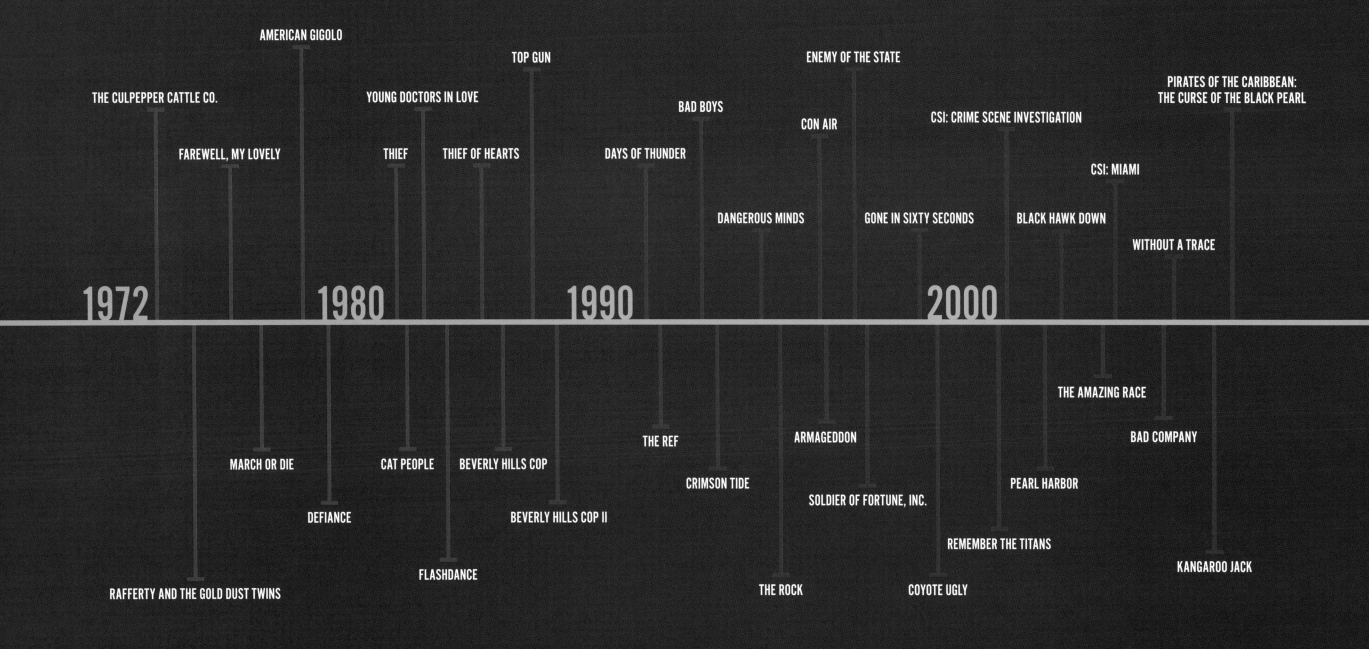

JERRY BRUCKHEIMER | FOUR DECADES OF FILMMAKING

AMERICAN GIGOLO

TOP GUN

ENEMY OF THE STATE

THE CULPEPPER CATTLE CO.

PIRATES OF THE CARIBBEAN:
THE CURSE OF THE BLACK PEARL

YOUNG DOCTORS IN LOVE

BAD BOYS

CSI: CRIME SCENE INVESTIGATION

CON AIR

FAREWELL, MY LOVELY

THIEF   THIEF OF HEARTS   DAYS OF THUNDER

CSI: MIAMI

DANGEROUS MINDS   GONE IN SIXTY SECONDS   BLACK HAWK DOWN

WITHOUT A TRACE

1972   1980   1990   2000

THE AMAZING RACE

THE REF   ARMAGEDDON   BAD COMPANY

MARCH OR DIE   CAT PEOPLE   BEVERLY HILLS COP

CRIMSON TIDE   PEARL HARBOR

DEFIANCE   BEVERLY HILLS COP II   SOLDIER OF FORTUNE, INC.

REMEMBER THE TITANS

KANGAROO JACK

FLASHDANCE

THE ROCK   COYOTE UGLY

RAFFERTY AND THE GOLD DUST TWINS

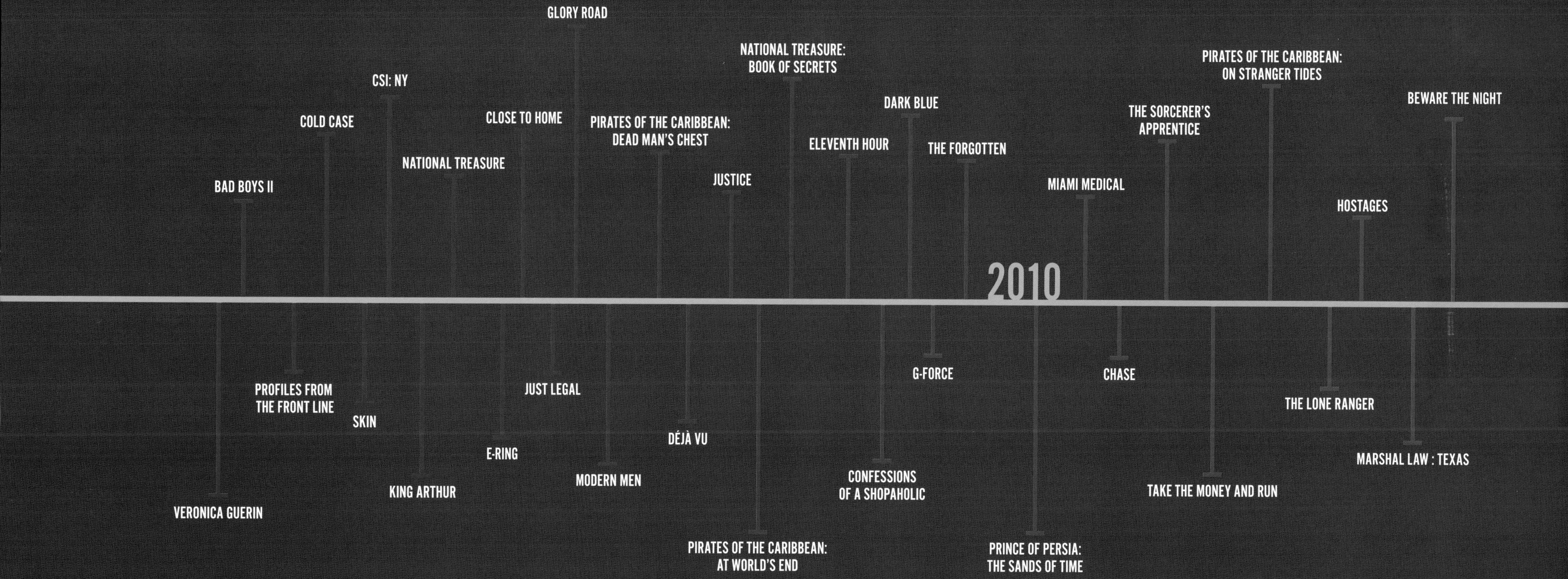

GLORY ROAD

NATIONAL TREASURE:
BOOK OF SECRETS

CSI: NY

PIRATES OF THE CARIBBEAN:
ON STRANGER TIDES

DARK BLUE

BEWARE THE NIGHT

COLD CASE

CLOSE TO HOME

PIRATES OF THE CARIBBEAN:
DEAD MAN'S CHEST

THE SORCERER'S
APPRENTICE

NATIONAL TREASURE

ELEVENTH HOUR

THE FORGOTTEN

BAD BOYS II

JUSTICE

MIAMI MEDICAL

HOSTAGES

2010

G-FORCE

CHASE

PROFILES FROM
THE FRONT LINE

JUST LEGAL

THE LONE RANGER

SKIN

E-RING

DÉJÀ VU

CONFESSIONS
OF A SHOPAHOLIC

TAKE THE MONEY AND RUN

MARSHAL LAW : TEXAS

KING ARTHUR

MODERN MEN

VERONICA GUERIN

PIRATES OF THE CARIBBEAN:
AT WORLD'S END

PRINCE OF PERSIA:
THE SANDS OF TIME

Image of Jerry Bruckheimer and Alexandra Balahoutis on page 34 © Alberto E. Rodriguez/WireImage

Image of Emmy Awards on page 269 © Kevork Djansezian/Getty Images

Academy Award® and Oscar® are registered trademarks of the Academy of Motion Picture Arts and Sciences.

BAFTA Award © British Academy of Film and Television Arts.

Emmy and the Emmy Statuette are the trademark property of ATAS/NATAS.

For information address Disney Editions, 1101 Flower Street Glendale, CA 91201 10011-5690.

Editorial Director: Wendy Lefkon

Editor: Jessica Ward

Design & Art Direction by John Sabel / Barry Grimes

ISBN 978-1-4231-3069-7
H106-9333-5-12001
Printed in Malaysia
First Edition
10 9 8 7 6 5 4 3 2 1

DISNEP EDITIONS
New York • Los Angeles

D23
The Official Disney Fan Club
Disney.com/D23

AUTHOR ACKNOWLEDGMENTS

Covering the entire life and career of a legendary producer in one volume was a glorious if daunting task, and I have been fortunate in having received much help along the way from innumerable friends and associates over the past five years since this book was first devised in October 2008. It is difficult to know where to start, and where to end in expressing so much gratitude, but I must obviously begin with the subject of this book: Jerry Bruckheimer, whose trust and support never ebbed. And to Linda Bruckheimer, not only for her wonderful contribution to the book, but also her expert guidance and advice. To Johnny Depp, mere thanks are not enough for providing such a wonderfully incisive Foreword; and also to Christi Dembrowski, Stephen Deuters, and Erik Schmudde at Infinitum Nihil. Much gratitude to everyone at Jerry Bruckheimer Films, including Mike Stenson, Chad Oman, Melissa Reid, Jill Weiss, Pat Sandston, Charlie Vignola, John Campbell, former archivist Jenny Cashman, and current archivist Emily Lewis, who helped unearth treasures from the past. Equal thanks to Jonathan Littman, KristieAnne Reed, and Mike Azzolino at Jerry Bruckheimer Television. To the brilliant designers, John Sabel and Barry Grimes; and to Jonathan Glick for his early contributions. Thanks to Jessica Bardwil, Dale Kennedy, Christopher O'Connell, Jeffrey Sotomayor, and Leslie Stern at Disney Franchise Management, and to Fredi Edwards, Laurence Schroeder, and Holly Clark in Disney Global Materials. Also, great appreciation to Jon Rogers, who was there at the beginning and helped spirit this project almost to the finish line, and to Marielle Henault. At Disney Publishing, I'm indebted to my wonderful (and patient) editor, Jessica Ward, as well as Jennifer Eastwood, Matthew Frank, Wendy Lefkon, Steffeni Lum, Warren Meislin, and Marybeth Tregarthen. Much gratitude and honor to Elizabeth Rudnick for her guidance at the beginning of the process, and to Karen Falzone for helping with an avalanche of clearances. And at Disney Legal, thanks to Margaret Adamic, Steve Borell, Betsy Mercer, Steve Plotkin, and Muriel Tebid. And to Paul Bloch and Chris Lebenzon for taking the time to provide new insights into a man they have known and worked with so much longer than I have. Thanks to everyone, past and present, who contributed their words, thoughts, and photographs, to this book, with a special nod to Stephen Berkman. And certainly not least, to my wife, Yuko Kikuchi Singer, and our daughters Miya and Kimi, whose love and support sustain me in all of my endeavors, and are always there to push me just a few more steps forward.

Michael Singer
Los Angeles, California
March 2013

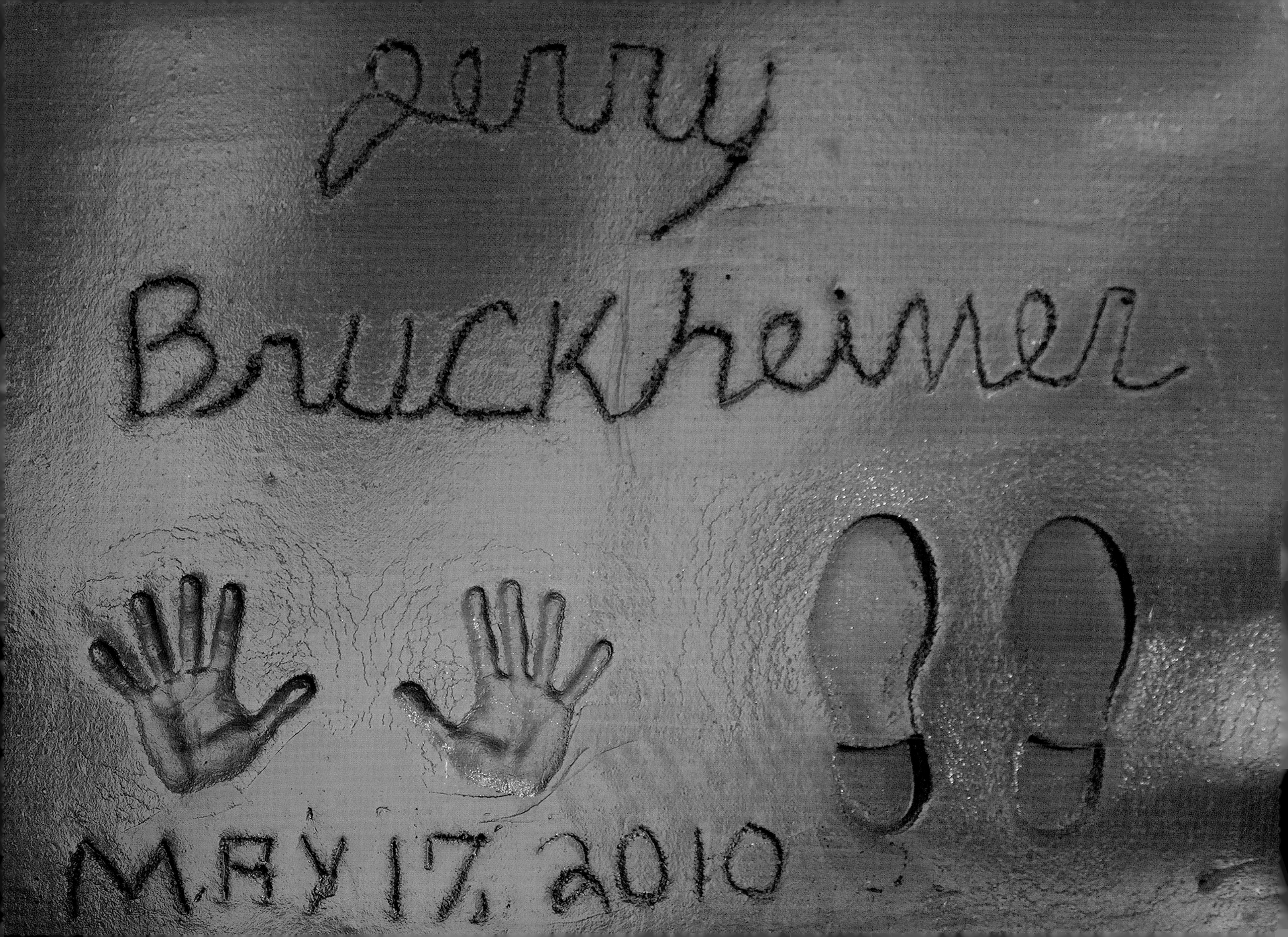
Jerry
Bruckheimer
MAY 17, 2010